ideals

Mama D's Italian
COOKBOOK

by Giovanna D'Agostino

Introduction

As a young bride, Giovanna D'Agostino, better known as Mama D, learned to cook in the same manner as her Italian landlady and sisters-in-law—with a "pinch of this and a pinch of that." This method of cooking soon developed into a desire to experiment and expand her cooking knowledge. With the concepts of good cooking fully learned, Mama D went on to create her own versions of traditional Italian fare which now entice members of her family, patrons of Sammy D's restaurant in Minneapolis, and a large following of good cooks who have delighted in Mama D's many personal appearances.

Mama D espouses a philosophy of cooking taste-tempting, nourishing food, prepared without the fanfare, but with all of the fine flavor of gourmet cooking. Her "waste not, want not" methods are a welcome aid in cooking delicious, but economical dishes. So, sample a full menu of Mama D's recipes, and you will be certain to return to her *Italian Cookbook* time after time.

Publisher, James Kuse
Managing Editor, Ralph Luedtke
Production Manager, Mark Brunner
Photo Editor, Gerald Koser
Copy Editor, Norma Barnes
Cookbook Editor, Julie Hogan
Photo Stylist, Rose Ann Pfeifer

Contents

Dedication

I would like to thank the many dear Italian ladies who taught me how to cook, especially my former landlady, Mrs. Roy Cinquegrani and my sisters-in-law, Rosina and Felicia.

ISBN 0-89542-623-4 295

Appetizers and Soups

"If the right seasonings are used, you can learn to cook without a measuring cup."

Pickled Zucchini

- 4 medium zucchini, sliced
- 2 cloves garlic, minced
- ½ cup chopped celery
- 1 medium onion, chopped
- 1 teaspoon salt
- ¼ teaspoon pepper
- ¼ teaspoon oregano
- ¼ cup wine vinegar
- ½ cup vegetable oil
- 1 bay leaf

Combine all ingredients, except vinegar and oil, in a bowl. Combine oil and vinegar and pour on above mixture. Toss lightly. Add bay leaf. Cover and refrigerate for eight hours or overnight. Serve as is or on lettuce. Serves 4 to 6.

Italian Pasties

- 2½ cups flour
- 1 teaspoon salt
- 1 cup lard
- 2 eggs
- 1 tablespoon vinegar
- 8 tablespoons water

Combine flour and salt in a mixing bowl. Cut in lard. Add eggs, vinegar and water. Mix to the consistency of pie dough. Roll into balls 1½ inches in diameter. Roll dough into circles on a lightly floured board. Place a spoonful of Filling on each. Fold dough over to the edge. Seal edges with fork tines. Place on a lightly greased baking sheet. Bake at 375° for thirty to forty minutes or until golden brown. Serves 4 to 6.

Filling

- 2 cups ricotta cheese
- 1 teaspoon salt
- ¼ teaspoon pepper
- ¼ teaspoon oregano
- ¼ teaspoon garlic powder
- 1 teaspoon minced parsley
- 2 eggs
- 3 slices salami, cut into small pieces
- 1 small onion, minced
- 3 slices mozzarella cheese, cut into small pieces

Mix all ingredients thoroughly in a large mixing bowl.

Fried Zucchini Flowers

- 16 zucchini flowers
- 2 eggs
- 1½ cups flour
- 1 teaspoon salt
- ¼ teaspoon pepper
- ¼ teaspoon oregano
- ¼ teaspoon garlic powder
- ¼ cup grated Romano cheese
- ½ cup water
- 2 cups vegetable oil

Remove pistils (centers) of flowers. Cut flowers in small pieces. Place all ingredients, except oil, in a medium-size mixing bowl. Beat until the mixture is the consistency of pancake batter. Add more flour or water if necessary. Heat oil in a large frying pan. Add batter a spoonful at a time and fry until golden brown. Garnish with additional Romano cheese before serving. Serves 4.

Chicken Wings

- 2 cups bread crumbs
- ½ cup grated Romano cheese
- 1 teaspoon salt
- ¼ teaspoon pepper
- ¼ teaspoon oregano
- ¼ teaspoon garlic powder
- 16 chicken wings
- Vegetable oil

Combine bread crumbs, cheese, salt, pepper, oregano and garlic powder. Dip wings first in oil, then in bread crumb mixture. Place wings on baking sheet and bake at 350° for one hour. Serves 4.

Pickled Mushrooms

- ½ pound fresh mushrooms, sliced
- 2 medium onions, thinly sliced
- 2 cups chopped celery
- 1 teaspoon salt
- ¼ teaspoon pepper
- ¼ teaspoon oregano
- ¼ teaspoon garlic powder
- ½ cup vegetable oil
- ¼ cup wine vinegar

Place mushrooms, onions and celery in a bowl. Season with salt, pepper, oregano and garlic powder. Combine oil and vinegar. Pour over mushrooms. Toss gently and refrigerate overnight. Serves 4.

Appetizers and Soups

"Fine gourmet cooking is done by the person who cooks simple and tasty food, dishes which are not necessarily made with exotic ingredients or an elaborate, intricate cooking process."

Italian Fried Mushrooms

    1 cup flour
    1 egg
    1 teaspoon salt
    ¼ teaspoon pepper
    ¼ teaspoon oregano
    ¼ teaspoon garlic powder
    ½ cup water
    ¼ cup grated Romano cheese
    1 pound mushrooms, cleaned
    2 cups vegetable oil
    1 egg, beaten with 2 tablespoons water

Combine flour, egg, salt, pepper, oregano, garlic powder, water and cheese in a large bowl. Mix well until the consistency of pancake batter. Heat oil in a small frying pan. Dip mushrooms in egg mixture, then in batter. Fry a few at a time until golden brown. Serves 4.

Antipasto Tray

    1 8-ounce carton French onion dip,
      or your choice
      Lettuce leaves
    8 slices salami, cut in half
    ½ pound Provolone cheese, cut into cubes
   16 pitted green olives
    4 thin slices ham, cut in half
    2 ribs celery, cut into 2-inch pieces
    2 large carrots, peeled and cut into sticks
    1 small head cauliflower
      broken into flowerets

Place dip in a small bowl in the center of an oblong platter. Cover the bottom of the platter with lettuce leaves. Fill celery with remaining dip. Place salami on one end of the platter and arrange remaining cheese, meat and vegetables in a circle around salami. Serves 6 to 8.

Prosciutto e Melone

    1 cantaloupe
    ½ pound thinly-sliced prosciutto ham

Remove seeds and rind from cantaloupe. Cut cantaloupe in wedges. Wrap prosciutto ham around each wedge. Place wedges on toothpicks. Serves 4.

Chicken Liver Paté

    1 pound chicken livers
    2 small onions, minced
    1 teaspoon minced parsley
    2 hard-cooked eggs, minced
    1 teaspoon salt
    ¼ teaspoon pepper
    ¼ teaspoon oregano
    ¼ teaspoon garlic powder
    3 tablespoons butter, softened

Put livers in a medium-size saucepan and cover with water. Bring water to a boil and cook for twelve minutes. Drain and chop fine. Put chopped liver in a bowl with onions, parsley, eggs, salt, pepper, oregano and garlic powder. Add butter and blend well. Place in a serving bowl and chill thoroughly. Serve with an assortment of crackers. Serves 4.

Italian Chicken Consomme

    4 cups chicken broth
    4 eggs
    ½ cup grated Parmesan cheese

Heat soup and ladle into bowls. Break one egg into each bowl. Sprinkle with cheese. Serves 4.

Whiting Fish Soup

    1 pound white fish
    3 tablespoons vegetable oil
    1 tablespoon butter
    2 cloves garlic, minced
    2 medium onions, chopped
    2 carrots peeled, cut into small pieces
    2 ribs celery, chopped
    2 medium potatoes, peeled and cubed
    2 quarts hot water
    2 tomatoes, crushed or chopped
 1½ teaspoons salt
    ¼ teaspoon pepper
    1 bay leaf
    ½ pound flat noodles
      Grated Parmesan cheese
      Lemon wedges

Rub salt on all sides of fish. Heat oil and butter in a large, deep pan. Add garlic, onions, carrots, celery, and potatoes and cook for ten minutes over low heat. Add water, tomatoes, salt, pepper, bay leaf and fish. Reduce heat and cook for twenty minutes. Remove fish to a platter. Add noodles and cook until tender. Ladle into soup bowls and sprinkle with Parmesan cheese. Garnish fish with lemon wedges. Serves 4 to 6.

"I have always made it a point to use ingredients that are easy to get, instead of those found only in odd corners of the spice shop."

Fish Soup

- 1½ pounds fish (sole, halibut, trout, or salmon) cleaned and cut into pieces
- ¼ cup vegetable oil
- ¼ cup butter
- 2 medium onions, finely chopped
- 2 cloves garlic, minced
- 1½ teaspoons salt
- ¼ teaspoon pepper
- ¼ teaspoon oregano
- ¼ teaspoon saffron
- 2½ cups water
- 2½ cups white wine
- ¼ cup grated Romano cheese

Heat oil and butter in a large saucepan. Add onions and garlic and sauté until onions are transparent. Add salt, pepper, oregano and saffron. Add fish and stir well. Add water and wine. Bring to a boil and then reduce heat. Simmer for twenty to twenty-five minutes. Ladle into soup bowls and sprinkle on grated cheese. Serves 4 to 6.

Beef Vegetable Soup

- 1 pound ground beef
- ¼ cup vegetable oil
- 4 potatoes, peeled and cubed
- 2 medium onions, chopped
- 6 carrots, sliced
- 2 cups diced celery
- ½ cup raw rice
- 2½ teaspoons salt
- ¼ teaspoon pepper

Heat oil in a large frying pan and sauté beef until browned. Place beef and three quarts of water in a large kettle and bring to a boil. Add potatoes, onions, carrots, celery, rice, salt and pepper. Reduce heat and simmer for two hours. Serves 6 to 8.

Chicken Soup with Pastina

- 2 pounds chicken wings, backs and necks
- 2 small onions, chopped
- 3 carrots, peeled and sliced
- 3 ribs celery, diced
- 1½ teaspoons salt
- ¼ teaspoon pepper
- 1 large potato, diced
- 2 tomatoes, crushed
- 1 pound pastina, prepared according to package directions and drained

Place chicken in a six-quart pan. Cover with water and bring to a boil. Skim fat. Add onions, carrots, celery, salt, pepper, potatoes and tomatoes. Reduce heat and simmer for two hours. Strain broth. Return vegetables to pan and add cooked pastina. Serves 6 to 8.

Minestrone with Ground Beef

- ¼ cup vegetable oil
- 1 pound ground beef
- 2 medium onions, minced
- 2 cloves garlic, minced
- 2 tablespoons minced parsley
- 1 16-ounce can tomatoes or 3 fresh tomatoes, crushed
- 2 ribs celery, diced
- 1 7-ounce can peas, drained
- 1 7-ounce can green beans, drained
- 2 carrots, peeled and diced
- 2 potatoes, peeled and sliced
- ½ cup grated Romano cheese

Heat oil in a large saucepan. Add meat, onions, garlic and parsley. Sauté until meat is lightly browned. Add tomatoes and cook for ten minutes over low heat. Fill a six-quart kettle two-thirds full of water and bring to a boil. Add celery, peas, beans, carrots and potatoes. Add tomato mixture and simmer for two hours. Ladle into bowls and top each with cheese. Serves 6.

Garbanzo Soup

- ½ pound salt pork
- ¼ cup vegetable oil
- 1 small onion, chopped
- 2 cloves garlic, minced
- 2 teaspoons minced parsley
- 2 tablespoons tomato sauce
- 2½ cups garbanzos or chick peas, undrained
- 1½ teaspoons salt
- ¼ teaspoon pepper
- 2 quarts water
- 1 pound any small pasta, prepared according to package directions and drained
- ½ cup grated Romano cheese

Cut up salt pork. Heat oil in soup kettle. Add salt pork, onions, garlic and parsley. Sauté until onions are transparent. Add tomato sauce, chick peas in liquid, salt and pepper. Add water and bring to a boil. Reduce heat and cook for thirty minutes. Add pasta to soup. Sprinkle with cheese and serve. Serves 4 to 6.

Salads

Shrimp and Potato Salad

  8 large potatoes, peeled, cooked and sliced
  2 hard-cooked eggs, chopped
  ½ cup sliced pitted black olives
  1 stalk celery, chopped, including leaves
  1 green onion, sliced
  ½ teaspoon salt
  ¼ teaspoon pepper
  4 tablespoons wine vinegar
  1 tablespoon vegetable oil
  6 tablespoons vinegar
  2 tablespoons vegetable oil
  1 pound shrimp, cleaned, deveined and cooked
    Lettuce leaves
    Hard-cooked eggs to garnish

Combine potatoes, eggs, olives, celery, onion and seasonings in a medium-size bowl. Combine four tablespoons wine vinegar and one tablespoon oil. Drizzle over above mixture. Toss lightly. Chill thoroughly. Chop all but eight of the shrimp. Combine vinegar and remaining oil and drizzle over shrimp. Refrigerate for several hours. Add chopped shrimp to potato salad mixture. Serve on lettuce leaves garnished with remaining shrimp and hard-cooked eggs, if desired. Serves 4 to 6.

Italian Tuna Fish Salad

  1 6½-ounce can tuna fish, drained and flaked
1½ cups diced celery
  1 green pepper, chopped
  2 hard-cooked eggs, cut lengthwise
    into wedges
  1 medium onion, chopped
  ½ cup sliced, pitted black olives
  ½ teaspoon salt
  ¼ teaspoon pepper
  ¼ teaspoon oregano
  ¼ cup grated Romano cheese
  1 tomato, cut in wedges
  ½ cup vegetable oil
  ¼ cup vinegar
    Lettuce

In a large bowl lightly toss all ingredients, except tomato, lettuce, vinegar and oil. Mix vinegar and oil together and pour over vegetables. Toss lightly. Place on lettuce beds and garnish with tomato wedges. Serves 4.

Macaroni with Prosciutto

  1 cup elbow macaroni
  4 tomatoes
  1 cup diced cucumber
  1 cup diced prosciutto ham
  1 tablespoon grated onion
  1 tablespoon minced parsley
  6 tablespoons vinegar
  2 tablespoons vegetable oil
  ½ teaspoon salt
  ¼ teaspoon pepper
  ½ teaspoon garlic powder
  ½ cup grated Parmesan cheese

Prepare macaroni according to package directions and drain. Cut tops off tomatoes and scoop out pulp. Place cucumber, prosciutto, onion and parsley in a medium-size bowl. Combine vinegar and oil. Drizzle over salad. Sprinkle on seasonings. Toss lightly. Spoon into tomato shells. Sprinkle with cheese. Serves 4.

Bagna Cauda

  1 stalk celery, cut into 2-inch pieces
  2 green peppers, julienned
  3 carrots, julienned
  1 small head cauliflower, broken into flowerets
  8 cherry tomatoes
  8 scallions, washed and trimmed
  8 mushrooms, wiped clean
  ½ cup vegetable oil
  ½ cup butter
  2 cloves garlic, minced
  1 teaspoon pepper
  6 anchovies, minced

Wash all vegetables and place in a large bowl with ice. Refrigerate until needed. Place oil, butter, garlic, pepper and anchovies in top of a double boiler and heat thoroughly. Cover and reduce heat. Simmer for fifteen minutes. Arrange vegetables on a serving platter. Pour heated butter mixture into individual bowls and allow guests to dip their own vegetables. Serves 4 to 6.

Salads

Italian Potato Salad

 8 medium potatoes, peeled, boiled and cubed
 2 medium onions, chopped
 2 cloves garlic, minced
 3 hard-cooked eggs, sliced
 1 teaspoon salt
 ¼ teaspoon pepper
 ½ cup vegetable oil
 ¼ cup vinegar
 ¼ cup grated Romano cheese

Place potatoes in a large bowl. Add onions, garlic and eggs. Season with salt, pepper and oregano. Mix lightly. Mix oil and vinegar together and pour over salad. Mix lightly. Sprinkle cheese over all and toss gently. Serves 4.

Squid Salad

1½ pounds squid
 1 cup chopped celery
 2 cloves garlic, minced
 1 tablespoon chopped parsley
 1 tablespoon lemon juice
 3 tablespoons vegetable oil
 1 tablespoon vinegar
 1 teaspoon salt
 ¼ teaspoon pepper
 ½ teaspoon oregano
 1 tablespoon grated Romano cheese

Remove tentacles, ink sac and skin from squid. Wash thoroughly. Cook for ten to twelve minutes in two quarts of boiling water. Drain. Cut into one-half inch rings. Place squid in a salad bowl. Add celery, garlic, parsley, lemon juice, oil, vinegar, salt, pepper and oregano. Mix well. Sprinkle on Romano cheese. Serves 4.

Shells with Mustard Greens

 1 pound shell macaroni, prepared according to package directions and drained
 1 pound mustard greens, cleaned
 ¼ cup vegetable oil
 2 cloves garlic, minced
 1 teaspoon salt
 ¼ teaspoon pepper
 ¼ teaspoon oregano

Bring water to a boil in a six-quart kettle. Add mustard greens and cook for five to seven minutes. Drain, reserving one cup of the cooking liquid. Heat oil in a large saucepan. Add garlic and sauté for three minutes. Add mustard greens, reserved cooking liquid, salt, pepper and oregano. Mix lightly. Stir in cooked pasta and reduce heat. Simmer for three to five minutes. Serves 4.

Italian Salad

 1 head bibb lettuce
 1 head romaine lettuce
 1 head iceberg lettuce
 1 avocado, diced
 1 green pepper, sliced
 1 small onion, minced
 8 radishes, sliced
 1 teaspoon salt
 ½ teaspoon pepper
 ½ teaspoon oregano
 ½ teaspoon garlic powder
1¼ cups vegetable oil
 ¼ cup wine vinegar
    Tomato wedges
 ½ cup grated Romano cheese

Clean all lettuce and tear into pieces. Place all vegetables in a large salad bowl. Season with salt, pepper, oregano and garlic powder. Mix oil and wine vinegar together in a bottle and drizzle over vegetables. Garnish with tomato wedges and Romano cheese. Serves 8.

Cauliflower Salad

 1 medium head cauliflower
 1 teaspoon salt
 ¼ teaspoon pepper
 ¼ teaspoon oregano
 ¼ teaspoon garlic powder
 2 cups diced celery
 6 tablespoons vegetable oil
 2 tablespoons wine vinegar
 2 tablespoons capers
 5 anchovies, cut up
10 pitted black olives, chopped

Cook cauliflower in boiling salted water until tender. Drain and break into flowerets. Place flowerets and stems in a bowl. Sprinkle with salt, pepper, oregano and garlic. Add celery. Mix oil and vinegar together in a bottle and pour over all. Toss lightly. Garnish with capers, anchovies and olives. Serves 4.

Baccala Salad

- 1 pound baccala (cod fish), cleaned
- ¾ teaspoon salt
- ¼ teaspoon pepper
- ¼ teaspoon oregano
- 2 cloves garlic, minced
- 8 large green olives
- 1 small onion, minced
- 1 red or green pepper, julienned
- ½ lemon
- ¼ cup vegetable oil
- 1 tablespoon vinegar

Boil fish in a large kettle of water until flaky and tender; drain. Place in a salad bowl and season with salt, pepper, oregano and garlic. Add olives, onions and peppers. Squeeze on lemon juice. Sprinkle with oil and vinegar. Toss lightly. Serves 4.

Olive, Egg and Potato Salad

- 4 eggs, hard-cooked and sliced
- 5 potatoes, peeled, boiled and cubed
- 1 cup chopped celery
- 2 medium onions, chopped
- ¼ cup grated Romano cheese
- 2 cloves garlic, minced
- 3 teaspoons chopped parsley
- 12 pitted black olives, sliced
- 1½ teaspoons salt
- ¼ teaspoon pepper
- ¼ teaspoon oregano
- 2 teaspoons wine vinegar
- 7 teaspoons vegetable oil

Combine eggs, potatoes, celery, onions, cheese, garlic, parsley and olives. Season with salt, pepper and oregano. Toss gently. Combine wine vinegar and oil in a bottle. Drizzle over salad and mix well. Serves 4 to 6.

Salada Miste

- 2 cups cooked string beans
- 1 medium onion, thinly sliced
- 1 cup cubed mozzarella cheese
- ½ cup thinly sliced pepperoni
- 2 cloves garlic, minced
- 1 teaspoon salt
- ¼ teaspoon pepper
- ¼ teaspoon oregano
- 4 tablespoons vegetable oil
- 1½ tablespoons wine vinegar
- ¼ cup grated Romano cheese

Place first five ingredients in a salad bowl. Season with salt, pepper and oregano. Toss lightly. Combine oil and vinegar. Pour over all ingredients. Sprinkle Romano cheese on top. Serves 4.

Hot Spinach Salad

- 2 cloves garlic, minced
  - Juice of 1 lemon
- 1 pound spinach, washed, drained, dried and torn into pieces
- 1 teaspoon salt
- ¼ teaspoon pepper
- ¼ teaspoon oregano
- ¼ cup vegetable oil
- ½ pound bacon, cut in small pieces
- 1 medium onion, sliced in rings
- 2 hard-cooked eggs, quartered

Heat oil in a large frying pan and fry bacon until crisp. Add garlic and lemon juice. Keep warm over low heat. Place spinach in a salad bowl. Season with salt, pepper and oregano. Pour bacon and oil over all. Garnish with onion and hard-cooked eggs. Serves 4.

Dandelion Salad

- 2 pounds dandelion greens
- 1 medium onion, chopped
- 1 clove garlic, minced
- 1 teaspoon salt
- ¼ teaspoon pepper
- ¼ teaspoon oregano
  - Wine vinegar
  - Vegetable oil

Wash greens and cut into thirds. Place in a salad bowl. Add onions, garlic, salt, pepper and oregano; toss lightly. Pour one-inch wine vinegar into a salad dressing bottle. Fill the rest of the bottle with oil to within one-inch of the top and shake. Drizzle dressing over salad. Toss salad lightly. Serves 4.

Insalata

- 5 medium tomatoes, sliced
- 1 medium cucumber, thinly sliced
- 1 green onion, thinly sliced
- 3 tablespoons olive oil
- 2 tablespoons wine vinegar
- ½ teaspoon salt
- ½ teaspoon oregano
- ¼ teaspoon basil
- ¼ teaspoon pepper
- 1 tablespoon minced parsley

Place tomatoes, cucumbers and onions in a large bowl. Combine remaining ingredients and mix lightly. Pour over salad. Chill well before serving. Serves 4 to 6.

Vegetables

Green Beans Almondine

    1 pound green beans, cleaned
    ¼ cup vegetable oil
    6 strips bacon, cut in pieces
    2 cloves garlic, minced
    1 medium onion, sliced
    ½ cup sliced almonds
    1 cup sliced mushrooms
    1 teaspoon salt
    ¼ teaspoon pepper
    ¼ teaspoon oregano
    ½ cup grated Romano cheese

Bring a three-quart pan of water to a boil. Add beans and cook for twenty minutes. Remove from heat and drain. Heat oil in a large frying pan. Add bacon, garlic and onions and sauté until onions are transparent. Add beans, almonds and mushrooms. Reduce heat and simmer for ten minutes. Stir in salt, pepper, oregano and cheese. Serves 4.

Spinach and Eggs

    ¼ cup vegetable oil
    1 pound fresh spinach, cleaned and cooked
    1 teaspoon salt
    ¼ teaspoon pepper
    ¼ teaspoon oregano
    ¼ teaspoon garlic powder
    ½ cup grated Romano cheese
    6 eggs, lightly beaten

Heat oil in a large saucepan. Add spinach, salt, pepper, oregano, garlic powder and cheese. Mix well. Add eggs and stir until eggs are cooked. Serves 4.

Dandelion Stew

    2 pounds dandelion greens
    3 cloves garlic, minced
    1½ teaspoons salt
    ¼ teaspoon pepper
    ¼ teaspoon oregano
    ½ cup vegetable oil
    ½ cup grated Romano cheese

Wash greens thoroughly. Place in a large kettle of boiling salted water and cook until tender. Drain. Return to pan and add garlic, salt, pepper, oregano, oil and cheese. Toss lightly. Serves 4.

Stuffed Zucchini

    6 medium zucchini
    1 pound ground beef
    ½ cup grated Romano cheese
    3 eggs
    1½ cups cooked rice
    1 teaspoon salt
    ¼ teaspoon pepper
    ¼ teaspoon oregano
    ¼ teaspoon garlic powder
    1 15-ounce can tomato sauce
    ½ cup grated mozzarella cheese

Cut zucchini in half, lengthwise, and scoop out pulp with a spoon. Set shells aside. Place zucchini pulp in a large bowl. Add meat, cheese, eggs, rice, salt, pepper, oregano and garlic. Mix well. Fill zucchini shells. Place shells in a baking pan and spoon on tomato sauce. Bake at 375° for forty-five to sixty minutes or until zucchini is tender. Prior to removing zucchini from oven, sprinkle on mozzarella cheese and bake until cheese is melted. Serves 4 to 6.

Stuffed Tomatoes

    8 anchovies, cut into small pieces
    2 teaspoons capers
    1½ cups bread crumbs
    ½ cup grated Romano cheese
    1 teaspoon salt
    ¼ teaspoon pepper
    ¼ teaspoon oregano
    2 cloves garlic, minced
    8 firm tomatoes
    4 tablespoons vegetable oil

Place anchovies, capers, one cup of the bread crumbs, cheese, salt, pepper, oregano and garlic in a blender and mix lightly. Add one tablespoon oil and blend for two minutes. Cut tomatoes in half crosswise and scoop out pulp. Fill with above mixture. Sprinkle with remaining bread crumbs and drizzle oil over each tomato. Place tomatoes in a greased baking dish. Bake at 350° for thirty minutes. Serves 8.

Vegetables

Broccoli Roll-ups

- 1 to 1½ pounds broccoli
- 3 tablespoons flour
- 1½ cups milk
- ¼ cup butter, melted
- 8 thin slices ham
- ½ cup grated Romano cheese

Clean broccoli in cold water. Remove hard stems, break into spears and peel skin to flowerets. Bring two quarts of water to a rolling boil and cook broccoli for seven minutes. Drain. Combine flour and milk and slowly add to melted butter. Roll ham around broccoli spears and place in a shallow, buttered casserole. Pour butter and milk mixture over all. Sprinkle Romano cheese over all and bake at 375° for ten minutes. Serves 4.

Baked Cauliflower

- 1 medium head cauliflower
- ½ cup grated Romano cheese
- 1 cup bread crumbs
- 1 teaspoon salt
- ¼ teaspoon pepper
- ¼ teaspoon oregano
- ¼ teaspoon garlic powder
- 4 tablespoons vegetable oil

Break cauliflower into flowerets and cut stems into pieces. Place in a kettle of boiling salted water and cook for eight minutes. Drain. Place cauliflower in an oiled baking dish. Mix together cheese, bread crumbs, salt, pepper, oregano and garlic powder. Sprinkle over cauliflower. Drizzle oil over all. Bake at 375° for thirty minutes or until cauliflower is tender. Serves 4.

Stuffed Eggplant

- 2 medium eggplants
- ½ cup vegetable oil
- 2 medium onions, chopped
- 2 cloves garlic, minced
- 1 teaspoon salt
- ¼ teaspoon pepper
- ¼ teaspoon oregano
- 4 tablespoons chopped parsley
- 2 slices bread
  Water
- ½ cup grated Romano cheese
- 2 eggs
- 1½ cups tomato sauce

Cut each eggplant in half. Scoop out pulp, reserving shells. Cube eggplant pulp. Heat oil in a large saucepan. Add eggplant, onions, garlic, salt, pepper, oregano and parsley. Sauté until eggplant is soft. Pour mixture into a large bowl. Soak bread in a dish of water and squeeze out excess. Combine bread, cheese and eggs with eggplant mixture. Mix well. Fill eggplant shells. Put in a greased baking pan to which one-quarter inch water has been added. Pour tomato sauce over each eggplant. Cover with aluminum foil and bake at 375° for one hour. Serves 4.

Green Beans with Tuna Fish

- 1 pound fresh green beans, cleaned
- ¼ cup vegetable oil
- 1 teaspoon salt
- ¼ teaspoon pepper
- ¼ teaspoon oregano
- 2 cloves garlic, minced
- 1 6½-ounce can tuna fish, drained and flaked
- 3 hard-cooked eggs, halved lengthwise
- ¼ cup grated Romano cheese
- 1 teaspoon lemon juice

Cook beans in salted water until tender and drain. Place beans in a bowl. Add oil, salt, pepper, oregano and garlic and toss together lightly. Place beans on a serving platter. Spoon tuna over beans. Garnish with eggs. Sprinkle cheese over all; drizzle lemon juice over all and serve. Serves 4.

Italian Zucchini Chops

- 6 small zucchini, thinly sliced
- 1 12-ounce can beer
- 1 egg
- 4 tablespoons flour
- 1 teaspoon salt
- ¼ teaspoon pepper
- ¼ teaspoon oregano
- ¼ teaspoon garlic powder
- ½ cup grated Romano cheese

To make batter, pour beer in a large bowl. Add egg, flour, salt, pepper, oregano, garlic powder and cheese. Mix well. Let stand for five minutes. Heat one-inch cooking oil in a large frying pan. Dip zucchini in batter. Fry each slice on both sides to a golden brown. Drain on paper toweling. Serves 4 to 6.

Eggplant Rolls

- ½ cup vegetable oil
- 2 eggplants, sliced lengthwise into ¼-inch slices
- 2½ cups bread crumbs
- ½ cup grated Parmesan cheese
- 1 teaspoon salt
- ¼ teaspoon pepper
- ¼ teaspoon oregano
- ¼ teaspoon garlic powder
- ½ pound thinly sliced ham, cut into thirds
- 1 29-ounce can tomato sauce
- ½ cup grated mozzarella cheese

Heat oil in a large frying pan. Add eggplant and sauté on both sides until lightly browned. Combine bread crumbs, cheese, salt, pepper, oregano and garlic powder in a large bowl and mix lightly. Coat each slice of eggplant in bread crumb mixture. Place a slice of ham on each slice of eggplant and roll up. Place in a baking dish. Pour tomato sauce over all and bake at 375° for one hour. Five minutes prior to removing from oven, sprinkle on mozzarella cheese and return to oven until cheese is melted. Serves 4 to 6.

Spinach alla Romana

- 1 pound fresh spinach
- ½ cup water
- ¼ cup vegetable oil
- 1 teaspoon salt
- ¼ teaspoon pepper
- ¼ teaspoon oregano
- ¼ teaspoon garlic powder
- ¼ cup grated Romano cheese

Clean spinach thoroughly. Pour water in a large saucepan. Add spinach and cook over moderate heat for ten minutes. Add oil, salt, pepper, oregano and garlic powder. Simmer for three to four minutes to heat thoroughly. Sprinkle with cheese. Serves 4.

Potato Soufflé

- 3 tablespoons butter
- 4 tablespoons chopped onion
- 1 cup milk
- 2 tablespoons flour
  Salt and pepper to taste
- 2 eggs, separated
- 3 cups leftover mashed potatoes

Melt butter in a small saucepan. Add onions and sauté until transparent. Combine milk with flour and add to onions. Stir constantly until mixture is thickened. Add sauce and egg yolks to mashed potatoes and mix thoroughly. Beat egg whites until stiff. Fold into potatoes. Place in a greased baking dish and bake for twenty-five to thirty minutes at 350°. Serves 4.

Escarole with Skroodles

- 1½ to 2 pounds escarole
- 3 tablespoons vegetable oil
- 3 tablespoons butter
- ½ teaspoon pepper
- 1 teaspoon salt
- ¼ teaspoon oregano
- 1 pound skroodles, prepared according to package directions and drained
- ¼ cup grated Romano cheese

Clean escarole. Cook in boiling water until tender. Drain. Heat oil and butter in a large saucepan. Add escarole and seasonings. Add skroodles and toss gently. Sprinkle grated cheese on each serving. Serves 4 to 6.

John's Vegetarian Dish alla Chablis

- 2 tablespoons vegetable oil
- 3 tablespoons butter
- 2 medium onions, thinly sliced
- 1 pound mushrooms, sliced
- 3 green peppers, julienned
- 2 cloves garlic, minced
- 1 teaspoon salt
- ¼ teaspoon pepper
- ¼ teaspoon oregano
- ¼ cup Chablis wine
- 2 tablespoons milk
- 2 tablespoons flour

Heat oil and butter in a large frying pan. Add onions, mushrooms, green peppers and garlic and sauté until onions are transparent. Add salt, pepper and oregano. Stir. Reduce heat and add wine. Mix milk and flour together. Add to frying pan, stirring constantly until thickened. Serve over cooked rice or noodles. Serves 4.

"Leftover cooked pasta can be used in homemade soup. Macaroni is easily made into delicious salads."

Main Dishes/Beef

Roasting and Broiling Beef

Times given for roasting will vary according to the amount of marbling, shape of the meat and whether or not it is boned. Preheat the oven and always have meat at room temperature before cooking. Test for doneness by touching meat with your finger. If it feels soft, it is rare; hard, it is well-done. Medium meat is firm, but not hard. On an instant meat thermometer, rare meat registers 130°, medium, 160°, and well done, 180°.

To broil meat, preheat broiler. Grease the pan if meat is very lean. Use fat from the meat or vegetable oil. To prevent curling, score edges by making shallow cuts along the outside every two inches. The broiling pan is generally set three inches below the heating element. Cook on one side at least four minutes, or until meat is nicely browned. Test with your finger or a meat thermometer.

Roast Prime Rib of Beef

    1 small prime rib roast
    2 teaspoons salt
    1 teaspoon pepper
    ½ teaspoon oregano
    ½ teaspoon garlic powder
    6 carrots, peeled
    2 medium onions, chopped
    4 potatoes peeled, halved

Place beef in roasting pan, fat side up. Season with salt, pepper, oregano and garlic powder. Pour one-inch water into bottom of pan. Arrange vegetables around roast. Bake at 325° until beef is done.

Gypsy Steak

    4 6-ounce New York strip steaks
    1 teaspoon salt
    ¼ teaspoon pepper
    ¼ teaspoon oregano
    ¼ teaspoon garlic powder
    ¼ cup vegetable oil
    2 small onions, chopped
    4 eggs

Season each steak with salt, pepper, oregano and garlic powder. Place under broiler and broil to desired degree of doneness. While steaks are being broiled, heat oil in a small saucepan; add onions and sauté until transparent. While onions are being sautéed, carefully break eggs into a greased baking dish and bake at 350° until the whites are firm, about ten to twelve minutes. Spoon onions over steak and top each with a baked egg. Serves 4.

T-Bone Steak alla Italiano

    4 T-Bone steaks
       Vegetable oil
       Salt
       Pepper
       Oregano
       Garlic powder
    1 tablespoon butter
    2 cups whole mushrooms

Rub oil on both sides of steak. Season with salt, pepper, oregano and garlic powder. Place mushrooms and butter in a small saucepan. Sauté for five minutes. Broil steaks to desired degree of doneness. When steaks are done, spoon mushrooms over top. Serves 4.

Sicilian Steak

    4 sirloin steaks, 6- to 8-ounces each,
       cut into ½-inch strips
 1½ cups bread crumbs
    ¼ cup grated Romano cheese
    1 teaspoon salt
    ¼ teaspoon pepper
    ¼ teaspoon garlic powder
       Vegetable oil
    ¼ cup vegetable oil
    2 green peppers, julienned
 1½ cups cooked, sliced mushrooms
    ½ cup white wine

Flatten steak with a mallet. Combine bread crumbs, cheese, and half the salt, pepper, and garlic powder. Dip meat in oil and then into bread mixture. Heat one-quarter cup oil in a large frying pan and sauté steak on both sides until browned. Remove steak from pan and set aside. Add peppers and mushrooms and sauté until soft. Add steak to peppers and mushrooms and stir gently. Season with remaining salt, pepper, oregano and garlic powder to taste. Pour wine over all and simmer for five minutes over low heat. Serves 4.

"I have a special name for the four basic seasonings, the SPOGS, or salt, pepper, oregano and garlic. If these seasonings are used properly, then you can say, as I do, that the SPOGS do a very good job."

La Beef Parmesan

1½ pounds round steak
½ cup grated Parmesan cheese
1½ cups bread crumbs
 2 teaspoons salt
½ teaspoon pepper
½ teaspoon oregano
½ teaspoon garlic powder
 1 teaspoon minced fresh parsley
 2 eggs, lightly beaten
½ cup vegetable oil
 1 medium onion, chopped
 1 6-ounce can tomato paste
 1 6-ounce can water
   Sliced mozzarella cheese

Flatten meat with a mallet and cut into eight-inch strips. Mix cheese, bread crumbs, one teaspoon salt, one-quarter teaspoon pepper, one-quarter teaspoon oregano, one-quarter teaspoon garlic powder and parsley. Dip meat in egg and then in bread crumb mixture. Heat oil in a large frying pan. Brown meat on both sides until golden brown. Lay in a greased 8 x 10-inch baking dish. Add onions to frying pan and sauté until onions are transparent. Mix tomato paste with water and add to onions. Season with one teaspoon salt, one-quarter teaspoon pepper, one-quarter teaspoon oregano and one-quarter teaspoon garlic powder. Cook and stir for five minutes. Pour three-fourths of the sauce over meat. Place a slice of mozzarella cheese on each piece of steak. Pour remaining sauce over all and bake at 350° for forty-five minutes. Serves 4.

Sirloin Tips alla Italiano

1½ pounds sirloin tips
½ cup flour
¼ cup vegetable oil
 1 tablespoon butter
 2 green peppers, chopped
 2 small onions, chopped
 2 cloves garlic, minced
 1 8-ounce can mushrooms or
   1½ cups sliced fresh mushrooms
½ cup water
¼ cup Chablis wine

Cut sirloin tips in strips two inches long and one-half inch wide. Dredge tips in flour. Heat oil and butter in frying pan. Add tips and sauté until lightly browned. Add peppers, onions, garlic and mushrooms. Sauté until onions are transparent. Add water. Reduce heat. Stir in wine and cook for five additional minutes. Serve over cooked rice or noodles. Serves 4 to 6.

Pepper Steak

¼ cup vegetable oil
 1 pound sirloin steak, cut into 5-inch strips
 4 green peppers, julienned
 3 cloves garlic, minced
 2 medium onions, chopped
 1 cup sliced mushrooms
 1 teaspoon salt
¼ teaspoon pepper
¼ teaspoon oregano
 1 cup chopped tomatoes
 1 cup white wine
½ cup grated Romano cheese

Heat oil in a large saucepan. Add steak, green peppers, garlic, onions and mushrooms. Sauté until onions are transparent. Stir in salt, pepper and oregano. Add tomatoes and wine. Reduce heat and cook for thirty minutes, stirring occasionally, until meat is tender. Serve over a bed of rice or flat noodles. Sprinkle with Romano cheese before serving. Serves 4.

Tripe alla Milanese

1½ pounds tripe, cut into small squares
 2 tablespoons butter
 2 tablespoons vegetable oil
 1 medium onion, chopped
 1 6-ounce can tomato paste
 1 cup water
1¼ teaspoons salt
¼ teaspoon pepper
¼ teaspoon oregano
¼ teaspoon garlic powder
1½ cups cooked rice
½ cup grated Romano cheese

Place tripe in three quarts cold water and bring to a boil. Reduce heat, cover and cook for ninety minutes. Drain. Melt butter and oil in saucepan. Add tripe and onions and sauté for seven minutes. Mix tomato paste and water. Pour over tripe. Season with salt, pepper, oregano and garlic powder. Cover and cook for thirty minutes. Add rice and cheese and mix well. Serves 4.

Meat Loaf

1½ pounds ground beef
½ pound ground pork
1 teaspoon salt
¼ teaspoon pepper
2 cloves garlic, minced
¼ teaspoon oregano
3 eggs, lightly beaten
½ cup grated Romano cheese
1 teaspoon chopped parsley
4 thin slices ham
1 8-ounce can tomato sauce
4 slices mozzarella cheese

Combine beef, pork, salt, pepper, garlic, oregano, eggs, Romano cheese and parsley. Mix well. Place meat mixture on waxed paper and press out to form a one-inch thick rectangle. Place ham on top of meat. Roll up meat from the long side. Place in a greased 9 x 12-inch baking pan. Pour tomato sauce over top of meat loaf. Lay mozzarella cheese over top. Bake at 375° for approximately one hour or until meat is done. Cool for ten minutes before slicing. Serves 4.

Steak Sinatra

½ cup butter
½ cup red Vermouth wine
2 green peppers, julienned
1 small onion, chopped
1 cup sliced mushrooms
  Salt, pepper, oregano and garlic powder to taste
4 thin slices sirloin steak

Melt butter in a large frying pan. Add half of the wine. Add peppers, onions and mushrooms. When peppers are almost cooked, add steak and simmer for seven minutes. Add seasonings and remaining wine. Simmer for five minutes. Remove steak to platter and spoon on peppers, onions and mushrooms. Serves 4.

Round Steak Pizzarola

¼ cup vegetable oil
2 tablespoons butter
1½ pounds round steak
2 cloves garlic, minced
1 small onion, minced
1½ teaspoons salt
¼ teaspoon pepper
¼ teaspoon oregano
½ teaspoon basil
1 29-ounce can tomato sauce
¼ cup warm water
¼ cup grated Romano cheese

Flatten steak on both sides with a mallet. Cut into four serving pieces. Heat oil and butter in a large frying pan. Brown meat on both sides. Stir in garlic, onions, salt, pepper, oregano and basil. Stir in tomato sauce and water. Simmer for forty-five to sixty minutes. Stir in cheese. Serve over fettucine. Serves 4.

Tiella

1 cup water
4 medium potatoes, sliced
4 medium zucchini, sliced
2 small green peppers, diced
2 small onions, chopped
1 pound ground beef
1½ cups tomato sauce
¼ cup vegetable oil
1 teaspoon salt
½ teaspoon pepper
¼ teaspoon oregano
¼ teaspoon garlic powder
1 cup grated Romano cheese

Grease an 8 x 10-inch baking pan. Pour water in the bottom. Layer potatoes, zucchini, peppers, onions and ground beef. Repeat layers until all ingredients have been used. Pour tomato sauce over top and then drizzle oil on. Season with salt, pepper, oregano and garlic powder. Sprinkle cheese over top and bake at 325° for one hour or until vegetables are tender. Serves 4.

Saucy Meatballs

1 pound ground beef
1 small onion, chopped
2 cloves garlic, minced
½ cup finely chopped walnuts
2 eggs, lightly beaten
1 teaspoon salt
¼ teaspoon pepper
¼ teaspoon oregano

Mix all ingredients together in a large bowl. Form into small balls. Place on a lightly greased baking sheet and bake at 350° for twelve to fifteen minutes. Place meatballs in a chafing dish. Pour sauce over all and serve. Serves 4.

Sauce

1 cup catsup
2 tablespoons vinegar
½ cup firmly-packed brown sugar
½ cup water

Combine all ingredients in a small saucepan. Stir over medium heat until well-blended and thoroughly heated.

Main Dishes/Beef

"For Italian foods I generally suggest a dry wine, white or red, Italian or otherwise. Also, a sweet cordial or liqueur is served as an Italian custom."

Liver Meat Loaf with Ricotta

½ pound beef liver, chopped
2 slices bread
　　Water
½ pound ground veal
¼ cup water
2 teaspoons parsley
¼ cup grated Romano cheese
1 medium onion, minced
2 cloves garlic, minced
2 teaspoons salt
¼ teaspoon pepper
¼ teaspoon oregano
4 eggs
2 cups ricotta cheese
¼ cup vegetable oil

Soak bread in water and squeeze out excess. Combine liver, veal, bread, water, one teaspoon of the parsley, Romano cheese, onions, garlic, one teaspoon of the salt, pepper, oregano and two of the eggs. Mix well. Combine ricotta, one teaspoon of the parsley, the remaining two eggs, and one teaspoon of salt. Grease a baking dish or loaf pan and place half of the meat in it. Place ricotta filling on meat, then add the remaining meat mixture. Seal edges with oil to enclose ricotta. Bake at 350° for forty-five minutes or until meat is done. Serves 6.

Spadini

½ cup bread crumbs
¼ cup grated Romano cheese
1 teaspoon minced parsley
¾ teaspoon salt
¼ teaspoon pepper
¼ teaspoon oregano
¼ teaspoon garlic powder
4 slices rib-eye steak, ¼-inch thick
⅛ cup vegetable oil
2 slices ham, cut in half
2 slices Swiss cheese, cut in half
1 cup canned spaghetti sauce
½ cup grated mozzarella cheese

Mix bread crumbs, Romano cheese, parsley, salt, pepper, oregano and garlic powder. Dip steak in oil, then coat one side in bread crumbs and lay flat on a working surface. Place one-half slice ham and one-half slice cheese on each steak. Top each with a spoonful of the bread crumbs and then a spoonful of spaghetti sauce. Roll up steak in jelly-roll fashion. Place on an ovenproof platter and broil both sides until browned. Remove and put a spoonful of spaghetti sauce and one tablespoon mozzarella cheese on each piece. Place under broiler until cheese is melted. Serves 4.

Italian Beef Kabobs

½ cup vegetable oil
1 teaspoon salt
¼ teaspoon pepper
¼ teaspoon oregano
¼ teaspoon garlic powder
1½ pounds round steak, cut into cubes
12 cherry tomatoes
12 fresh mushrooms, cleaned
2 medium onions, cut in eighths
2 green peppers, cut into large pieces

Combine oil, salt, pepper, oregano and garlic powder in a large bowl. Mix thoroughly. Add beef cubes and mix lightly. Cover and allow steak to marinate for ninety minutes. Place steak alternately on skewers with tomatoes, mushrooms, onions and green peppers, ending with tomato. Place skewers on a flat baking sheet and broil until meat is the desired degree of doneness. Serve over rice. Serves 4.

Italian Beef Stroganoff

½ cup butter
2 pounds beef sirloin, cut into 1-inch pieces
2 medium onions, chopped
2 cloves garlic, minced
2 teaspoons minced parsley
¼ cup grated Romano cheese
½ pound mushrooms, sliced
2½ cups milk
3 tablespoons flour
1 teaspoon salt
¼ teaspoon oregano
¼ teaspoon pepper

Melt butter in a large frying pan. Add beef and brown lightly. Add onions and garlic and sauté over low heat for three minutes, stirring often. Stir in parsley, cheese and mushrooms, and cook for five minutes over low heat. Combine milk and flour and blend well. Stir milk into meat mixture. Add seasonings and heat thoroughly. Serve over noodles or rice. Serves 4.

Beef and Cabbage Casserole

    ¼ cup vegetable oil
    2 medium onions, chopped
    2 cloves garlic, minced
 1½ pounds ground beef
    ¼ cup grated Romano cheese
    1 teaspoon salt
    ¼ teaspoon pepper
    ¼ teaspoon oregano
    2 medium heads cabbage, cut in large pieces
    1 6-ounce can tomato sauce
    1 6-ounce can water
    ¼ cup shredded mozzarella cheese

Heat oil in a large frying pan. Add onions and garlic and sauté until onions are transparent. Add beef, Romano cheese, salt, pepper and oregano. Sauté until meat is lightly browned. Using a three-quart casserole, layer cabbage and meat mixture until all is used. Mix tomato sauce with water and pour over all. Sprinkle with mozzarella cheese and bake, uncovered, at 350° for ninety minutes. Serves 4.

Pastaccii

    ½ cup vegetable oil
    ½ cup butter
    2 medium onions, chopped
    2 cloves garlic, minced
    1 pound ground beef
    1 teaspoon salt
    1 teaspoon pepper
    ½ teaspoon nutmeg
    ½ teaspoon cinnamon
    2 15-ounce cans tomato sauce
    ½ cup white Chablis wine
    1 pound small macaroni
    3 eggs, lightly beaten
 1½ cups grated Romano cheese

Melt butter and oil in a large saucepan. Add onions and garlic and sauté for five minutes. Add meat and cook until browned. Add salt, pepper, nutmeg, cinnamon, tomato sauce and wine. Reduce heat and cook for one-half hour. Prepare macaroni according to package directions and drain. Place macaroni in a mixing bowl. Add eggs and three-quarters cup of cheese. Mix well. Butter a 9 x 12-inch baking pan. Place half of the macaroni in the pan. Top with meat sauce. Add another layer of macaroni and top with meat sauce. Sprinkle remaining cheese over all. Bake at 375° for thirty minutes. Serve with Bechamel Sauce (recipe on page 52).

Liver with Mushrooms

    ¼ cup vegetable oil
    5 strips bacon, cut into pieces
    2 medium onions, chopped
 1½ pounds liver, chopped
      Flour
 1½ cups sliced mushrooms
    1 teaspoon salt
    ¼ teaspoon pepper
    ¼ teaspoon oregano
    ¼ teaspoon garlic powder
    ½ cup water

Heat oil in a large frying pan. Add bacon and onions and sauté until onions are transparent. Remove onions and bacon from frying pan. Dredge liver in flour and brown on both sides. Spoon bacon and onions over liver. Add mushrooms, salt, pepper, oregano, garlic powder and water. Reduce heat and simmer for fifteen minutes or until liver is done. Serves 4.

Liver alla Veneziana

    ½ cup vegetable oil
    2 medium onions, chopped
    2 cloves garlic, minced
    1 tablespoon chopped parsley
    ½ cup flour
    1 pound liver, thinly sliced and cut into strips
    1 teaspoon salt
    ¼ teaspoon pepper
    ½ cup white wine

Heat oil in a large saucepan. Add onions, garlic and parsley and sauté until onions are transparent. Remove from pan and set aside. Dredge liver in flour. Sauté liver on both sides. Add onions, salt and pepper. Pour wine over all and simmer over low heat for fifteen minutes. Serves 4.

Liver and Rice Casserole

    ¼ cup vegetable oil
    2 tablespoons butter
 1½ pounds liver, chopped
    2 medium onions, minced
    2 cloves garlic, minced
    ½ cup tomato sauce
    1 teaspoon salt
    ¼ teaspoon oregano
    ¼ teaspoon pepper

Heat oil and butter in a small frying pan. Sauté liver, onions and garlic until onions are transparent. Add tomato sauce. Season with salt, oregano and pepper and simmer over low heat until liver is done. Spoon over Italian Rice Pilaf (recipe on page 41.) Serves 4.

Italian Ground Beef Casserole

    2 tablespoons butter
    2 tablespoons vegetable oil
    1 large onion, diced
    2 cloves garlic, minced
    1 green pepper, diced
    1 pound ground beef
    ½ cup tomato sauce
    3 medium potatoes, peeled and diced
    1 teaspoon salt
    ¼ teaspoon pepper
    ¼ teaspoon oregano
    2 cups cooked rice
    6 thin slices ham
    ½ cup water

Heat oil and butter in a large saucepan. Add onions, garlic, green pepper and ground beef. Sauté until onions are transparent. Add tomato sauce, potatoes, salt, pepper and oregano and cook over low heat for fifteen minutes. Place rice in a three-quart casserole. Lay ham over rice. Spoon ground meat mixture over ham. Add water. Bake at 375° for one-half hour. Serves 4 to 6.

Gaetano's Liver alla Kabob

    1 pound liver, cut into pieces
    2 medium onions, quartered
    ½ pound salt pork, cut into cubes
    1 6-ounce can tomato paste
    1 6-ounce can water

Alternately place liver, two pieces of onion and pork on a skewer until all ingredients are used. Combine tomato paste with water. Pour half of paste and water in the bottom of a baking dish large enough to hold skewers. Lay skewers in baking dish. Pour remaining tomato paste and water over skewers. Season with salt and paprika to taste. Place in oven and bake at 350° for twenty to twenty-five minutes. Serves 4.

Beef and Zucchini Casserole

    2 tablespoons vegetable oil
    1 pound ground beef
    3 cups bread crumbs
    ½ cup grated Romano cheese
    2 teaspoons salt
    ½ teaspoon pepper
    ½ teaspoon oregano
    ½ teaspoon garlic powder
    6 small zucchini, peeled and sliced
    4 potatoes, peeled and sliced
    2 medium onions, chopped
    3 green peppers, julienned
    ½ cup vegetable oil

Heat oil in a large frying pan and brown beef lightly. Mix together bread crumbs, cheese, one teaspoon salt, one-quarter teaspoon pepper, one-quarter teaspoon oregano and one-quarter teaspoon garlic powder. In a greased 8 x 10-inch baking dish layer zucchini, potatoes, onions and green peppers. Sprinkle bread crumbs over each layer. Repeat layers until all ingredients are used, ending with potatoes. Sprinkle oil over top layer. Bake, covered, at 375° for one hour or until potatoes are done. Serves 4.

Beef Stew No. 1

    ½ cup vegetable oil
    2 medium onions, chopped
    2 cloves garlic, minced
    2 cups sliced mushrooms
    1 2½- to 3-pound chuck roast, cut
        into 1-inch pieces
    ½ cup flour
    1 teaspoon salt
    ¼ teaspoon pepper
    ¼ teaspoon rosemary
    1 6-ounce can tomato paste
    1 6-ounce can water
    ½ cup red wine
    4 carrots, peeled and sliced
    4 medium potatoes, peeled and cubed

Heat oil in a large saucepan. Add onions, garlic and mushrooms. Sauté until onions are transparent. Dredge meat in flour and add to onion mixture. Brown meat on all sides. Season with salt, pepper and rosemary. Mix tomato paste with water; pour over meat. Stir in wine. Add carrots and potatoes. Cover and cook over low heat for two hours. Serves 4.

Beef Stew No. 2

    3 medium zucchini, sliced
    4 ribs celery, cut into pieces
    2 small onions, cut into pieces
    6 carrots, sliced
    4 potatoes, peeled and cubed
    1 pound beef stew meat, cut into chunks
    ¼ cup vegetable oil
    1 8-ounce can tomato sauce
    1 teaspoon salt
    ¼ teaspoon pepper
    ¼ teaspoon oregano
    ¼ teaspoon garlic powder
    ½ cup grated Romano cheese

Place all ingredients in a small roasting pan and mix well. Bake, covered, at 375° for seventy-five minutes or until meat and carrots are tender. Serves 4.

Main Dishes/Pork

Minestra

¼ cup vegetable oil
2 pounds pork or beef, cut in 1-inch pieces
2 medium onions, chopped
1 teaspoon salt
¼ teaspoon pepper
¼ teaspoon oregano
¼ teaspoon garlic powder
3 small tomatoes, cut into small pieces
5 carrots, peeled and cut into small pieces
4 potatoes, peeled and cut into small pieces
1 pound green beans, cut into small
　　pieces and cooked
1 cup water

Heat oil in a large frying pan. Add meat and brown lightly. Add onions, salt, pepper, oregano, garlic powder, tomatoes, carrots, potatoes and green beans. Stir in water and cook over low heat for one hour, or until done. Serves 4.

Pork and Zucchini Stew

¼ cup vegetable oil
1½ pounds pork roast, cut into 1-inch pieces
2 small onions, chopped
2 cloves garlic, minced
1 bay leaf
1 teaspoon salt
¼ teaspoon pepper
¼ teaspoon oregano
1 8-ounce can tomato sauce
½ cup red wine
3 potatoes, peeled and diced
4 medium zucchini, sliced

Heat oil in a Dutch oven. Add pork and sauté for seven minutes, stirring often. Add onions, garlic, bay leaf, salt, pepper and oregano. Sauté until onions are transparent. Add tomato sauce, wine, potatoes and zucchini. Cook over low heat for about one hour, or until meat is done. Serves 4.

Porchetta

1 4- to 5-pound pork loin roast, bone removed
2 teaspoons salt
¼ teaspoon pepper
¼ teaspoon oregano
2 cloves garlic, minced
2 teaspoons sage
2 teaspoons basil
1 bay leaf, crushed
1½ teaspoons rosemary

Mix all spices, using only one teaspoon of the salt. Spread spices on the inner side of the pork loin. Roll meat and tie securely with string. Place pork in a roasting pan. Add enough water to cover meat half way. Season top of meat with remaining salt. Bake at 350° for two hours or until meat is thoroughly cooked. Serves 4 to 6.

Sausage and Spaghetti Casserole

1 pound Italian sausage
¼ cup vegetable oil
1 medium onion, chopped
2 cloves garlic, minced
2 cups sliced mushrooms
1 29-ounce can tomato sauce
1 teaspoon salt
¼ teaspoon pepper
¼ teaspoon oregano
½ cup grated Romano cheese
1 pound spaghetti, prepared according to
　　package directions and drained
½ cup grated mozzarella cheese

Bake sausage at 350° for forty-five minutes. Cut into one-half inch pieces. Heat oil in a large frying pan and sauté onions, garlic and mushrooms for five minutes. Stir in tomato sauce, salt, pepper and oregano. Simmer for one hour. Place spaghetti in a four-quart casserole. Sprinkle on Romano cheese. Pour cooked tomato sauce on top. Sprinkle on mozzarella cheese. Bake at 375° for fifteen minutes or until cheese is golden. Serves 4.

Stuffed Pork Chops with Prosciutto

6 center-cut pork chops, sliced 1½-inches thick
½ cup chopped prosciutto ham
½ cup grated mozzarella cheese
¼ cup grated Romano cheese
1 cup bread crumbs
1 teaspoon salt
¼ teaspoon pepper
¼ teaspoon oregano
1 egg
½ cup vegetable oil
　　Paprika and salt to taste
½ cup water

Cut pockets in pork chops or have your butcher do it for you. Mix prosciutto, cheeses, bread crumbs, salt, pepper, oregano and egg. Fill pockets of pork chops with above mixture. Heat oil in a large frying pan and brown chops on both sides. Place in a covered baking dish and sprinkle with paprika and salt. Add water; cover and bake at 350° for one hour. Serves 4.

Baked Ham with Tomatoes and Cheese

    2 slices ham, 1-inch thick
2½ cups Italian plum tomatoes, drained and chopped
    ½ teaspoon salt
    ¼ teaspoon oregano
    ¼ cup grated Parmesan cheese

Place ham in a baking dish. Spoon on tomatoes. Sprinkle on seasonings. Cover baking dish with aluminum foil. Bake at 350° for forty-five minutes, or until ham is tender. Fifteen minutes before baking time is completed, uncover the dish and sprinkle on Parmesan cheese. Bake until cheese is melted. Serves 4.

Piemontese Pork

    ¼ cup butter
    2 tablespoons olive oil
1½ pounds pork tenderloin, thinly sliced and flattened
    ¾ cup white wine
    1 teaspoon salt
    ½ teaspoon oregano
    ½ teaspoon basil
    1 tablespoon parsley flakes
      Pepper to taste
      Sliced Provolone cheese

Heat butter and oil in a large frying pan. Add pork and brown well on both sides. Stir in wine, salt, oregano, basil, parsley and pepper. Simmer over low heat for fifteen minutes, basting frequently. Place pork in a shallow baking dish. Pour sauce from pan over all. Place Provolone cheese on each slice of pork. Bake at 400° for about twelve minutes, or until cheese melts. Serves 6.

Pork Stew

    ½ cup flour
    1 teaspoon salt
    ¼ teaspoon pepper
    2 pounds pork loin, cut into cubes
    4 tablespoons shortening
    4 cups hot water
    1 tablespoon lemon juice
    1 large onion, sliced
    1 bay leaf
  10 small carrots, peeled
    8 small potatoes, peeled
    1 small zucchini, peeled and sliced

Combine flour, salt and pepper. Coat pork cubes in flour mixture. Melt shortening over moderate heat in a Dutch oven. Brown pork on all sides and remove from Dutch oven. Add water. Stir in lemon juice, onion and bay leaf. Return meat to Dutch oven. Reduce heat, cover, and simmer for about two hours, or until meat is tender. Add carrots, potatoes, and zucchini and cook an additional twenty-five minutes, or until vegetables are tender. Serves 4.

Sausage and Ditali

    2 tablespoons vegetable oil
1½ pounds Italian sausage, cut into pieces
    2 medium onions, chopped
    ½ teaspoon garlic powder
    1 teaspoon salt
    ¼ teaspoon pepper
    1 10-ounce can tomato puree
    1 pound ditali
    ½ cup grated Parmesan cheese

Heat oil in a large frying pan. Add sausage and sauté for five to seven minutes. Add onions and garlic powder and sauté until onions are transparent. Add salt and pepper and mix well. Stir in tomato puree. Bring to a boil, reduce heat and cook for one hour, stirring occasionally. Prepare ditali according to package directions; drain. Mix ditali thoroughly with sauce and sprinkle with Parmesan cheese. Serves 4.

Pork Chop Casserole

    ¼ cup vegetable oil
    6 center-cut pork chops
    2 green peppers, chopped
    2 medium green onions, chopped
    ½ cup chopped celery
    1 cup raw rice
    2 cups tomato sauce
1½ teaspoons salt
    ¼ teaspoon pepper
    ¼ teaspoon oregano
    2 cloves garlic, minced
    ½ cup water
    ½ cup grated Romano cheese

Heat oil in a frying pan and brown chops on both sides. Place chops in a four-quart casserole and add green pepper, onions, celery, rice and tomato sauce. Sprinkle on salt, pepper, oregano and garlic. Add water. Sprinkle with cheese. Cover and bake at 375° for one hour. Serves 4.

Stuffed Pork Chops

    4 double-ribbed, center-cut pork chops
    4 slices bread
      Water
    2 eggs, lightly beaten
    ½ cup grated Romano cheese
    1 teaspoon minced parsley
    1 teaspoon salt
    ¼ teaspoon pepper
    ¼ teaspoon oregano
    ½ teaspoon garlic powder
    ¼ cup vegetable oil
    1 cup water

Cut pockets in pork chops or have your butcher do it for you. Soak bread in a dish of water and squeeze out excess. Combine bread, eggs, cheese, parsley, salt, pepper, oregano and garlic powder. Mix until well-blended. Fill pockets of pork chops with bread mixture. Heat oil in a large frying pan. Brown chops on both sides. Place chops in a buttered baking dish large enough to hold all. Add water and cover. Bake at 350° for one hour. Serves 4.

Eggplant with Sausage

    ½ cup vegetable oil
    1 large eggplant or 2 medium, sliced
    1½ cups bread crumbs
    ½ cup grated Romano cheese
    2 teaspoons salt
    ¼ teaspoon pepper
    ¼ teaspoon oregano
    2 tablespoons chopped parsley
    2 cloves garlic, minced
    1 pound ground pork
    2 small onions, minced
    2 teaspoons fennel
    3 hard-cooked eggs, sliced
    1½ cups tomato sauce
    ½ cup cubed mozzarella cheese

Heat oil in a large frying pan. Brown eggplant on both sides. Remove from pan and set aside. In a small bowl, mix bread crumbs, Romano cheese, one teaspoon salt, pepper, oregano, parsley and garlic. In a separate bowl, combine pork, onions, remaining salt and fennel, and mix well. Place pork mixture in the frying pan and sauté until crumbly. Grease an 8 x 10-inch baking pan. Layer eggplant, meat mixture, a few slices of egg and bread crumb mixture until all ingredients are used. Spread tomato sauce over top. Place mozzarella cheese over sauce. Cover with aluminum foil and bake at 350° for one hour. Serves 4 to 6.

Pork Chops alla Mama D

    3 tablespoons vegetable oil
    1 medium onion, chopped
    2 green peppers, chopped
    2 cloves garlic, minced
    ½ pound mushrooms, sliced
    6 center-cut pork chops
    ½ teaspoon salt
    ¼ teaspoon pepper
    ¼ teaspoon oregano
    1 bay leaf
    ½ teaspoon rosemary
    ½ cup white wine

Heat oil in a large frying pan. Add onions, peppers, garlic and mushrooms and sauté until onions are transparent. Add chops and brown on both sides. Add salt, pepper, oregano, bay leaf and rosemary. Stir in wine and cover. Cook over low heat for about twenty minutes, or until chops are cooked. Serves 6.

Polenta Casserole

Polenta

    1 teaspoon salt
    3½ cups water
    1 cup cornmeal
    1 cup cold water
    ½ cup grated Romano cheese

Add salt to water and bring to a boil. Gradually add cornmeal and cold water, stirring until thickened. Reduce heat and cover. Cook slowly for eight minutes, stirring frequently. Remove from heat. Place cornmeal on a serving platter. Spoon sausage mixture over top. Sprinkle with Romano cheese. Serves 4.

Sausage

    1 pound coarsely ground pork
    1 teaspoon fennel seed
    ⅛ teaspoon hot red pepper
    1 teaspoon salt
    3 tablespoons vegetable oil
    2 cups sliced mushrooms
    1 29-ounce can tomato sauce
    1 teaspoon salt
    ¼ teaspoon pepper

Mix first four ingredients thoroughly. Heat oil in a large saucepan. Add sausage and mushrooms. Saute until sausage is browned. Stir in tomato sauce, salt and pepper. Simmer for thirty-five minutes over low heat.

Veal al Grancessi

- 1 pound veal, thinly sliced
- 1 teaspoon salt
- ¼ teaspoon pepper
- ¼ teaspoon oregano
- ¼ teaspoon garlic powder
- 2 eggs
- ¼ cup milk
- 1¼ cups flour
- ½ cup vegetable oil
- 1 lemon, sliced

Pound veal with a mallet on both sides to flatten. Season with salt, pepper, oregano and garlic powder. Beat eggs and milk together. Dredge veal in flour, then in egg mixture and then in flour again. Heat oil in a large frying pan. Sauté veal on both sides. Cook over low heat until meat is done. Place veal on platter. Place lemon slices between pieces of veal. Garnish with parsley. Serves 4.

Veal Chops alla Pizzarola

- ½ cup vegetable oil
- 6 veal chops
- 1 medium onion, minced
- 2 cloves garlic, minced
- 1 teaspoon salt
- ¼ teaspoon pepper
- ½ teaspoon oregano
- 1 teaspoon minced parsley
- 1 15-ounce can tomato sauce
- ½ cup red wine

Heat oil in a large frying pan. Add chops and brown on each side. Add onions, garlic, salt, pepper, oregano, parsley and tomato sauce. Reduce heat and cook slowly for thirty minutes or until meat is tender. Add wine and cook for ten minutes. Serves 4.

Veal al Caruso

- 4 thin slices veal
- 2 cups bread crumbs
- ¼ cup grated Romano cheese
- 2 teaspoons minced parsley
- 1 teaspoon salt
- ¼ teaspoon pepper
- ¼ teaspoon oregano
- ¼ teaspoon garlic powder
- ¼ cup vegetable oil
- 4 slices eggplant, sautéed on both sides
- 4 slices mozzarella cheese
- 1 cup Meat Sauce (recipe on page 50)

Flatten veal with a mallet so that it is paper-thin. Mix bread crumbs, cheese, parsley, salt, pepper, oregano and garlic. Dip veal into oil; then dip into bread crumb mixture to coat both sides. Heat oil in a frying pan and sauté veal on both sides. Place veal on broiler pan and top with one slice eggplant, a small amount of sauce and a slice of cheese. Broil until cheese is melted. Serves 4.

Costolette

- 2 cups bread crumbs
- 1½ cups grated Romano cheese
- 1 teaspoon salt
- ¼ teaspoon pepper
- ¼ teaspoon oregano
- 2 cloves garlic, minced
- 2 teaspoons minced parsley
- ¼ teaspoon basil
- 6 veal chops, thinly sliced
- 2 eggs, lightly beaten
- ½ cup vegetable oil

Mix bread crumbs, cheese, salt, pepper, oregano, parsley and basil. Dip chops into egg, then into bread mixture. Heat oil in a large frying pan and sauté chops on both sides until golden brown. Serves 4.

Bracciole of Veal

- 2 cups bread crumbs
- ½ cup grated Romano cheese
- 1 tablespoon parsley flakes
- 1 teaspoon salt
- ¼ teaspoon pepper
- ¼ teaspoon oregano
- ¼ teaspoon garlic powder
- 1½ pounds veal, sliced into 6 pieces
- ¼ cup vegetable oil
- 6 slices ham
- 6 slices Swiss cheese
- ¾ cup tomato sauce
- Grated mozzarella cheese

Combine bread crumbs, Romano cheese, parsley, salt, pepper, oregano and garlic powder. Dip veal in oil, then coat both sides in bread mixture. Place a slice of ham and a slice of cheese on each piece of veal. Sprinkle a little of the bread mixture on top and roll each slice of veal. Place on a baking sheet and bake at 375° for twenty minutes. Prior to removing from oven, place a tablespoon of tomato sauce on each roll and sprinkle with mozzarella cheese. Bake until cheese melts. Serves 6.

Veal Franchaise

    4 tablespoons butter
1½ pounds thinly sliced veal, cut into 3-inch pieces
    Flour for dredging
    2 eggs, lightly beaten
    2 tablespoons white wine
    1 teaspoon lemon juice
    1 teaspoon salt

Melt butter in a large saucepan. Dredge veal in flour, then in eggs and again in flour. Sauté veal on each side until lightly browned. Combine wine, lemon juice and salt and add to veal. Reduce heat and simmer until veal is tender. Serve on a bed of Italian Rice Pilaf (recipe on page 41). Serves 4.

Veal Scallopinne

    ½ cup flour
    2 teaspoons salt
    ½ teaspoon pepper
    ½ teaspoon oregano
    ¼ teaspoon garlic powder
    1 pound thinly sliced veal, cut into 2-inch pieces
    ¼ cup vegetable oil
    2 tablespoons butter
    1 medium onion, chopped
    2 cloves garlic, minced
    1 2-ounce can capers
    1 cup sliced mushrooms
    2 teaspoons chopped parsley
    3 tomatoes

Combine flour, one teaspoon salt, one-quarter teaspoon pepper, one-quarter teaspoon oregano and garlic powder in a small bowl. Dredge veal in flour mixture. Heat oil and butter in a large frying pan. Sauté veal on both sides until golden brown. Remove veal and set aside. In the same frying pan, add onions and garlic and sauté until onions are transparent. Add capers, remaining salt, pepper and oregano, mushrooms and parsley; stir. Squeeze tomatoes by hand into frying pan. Add veal and stir. Cook over moderate heat until veal is tender, stirring often. Serves 4.

Veal Scallopinne alla Marsala

    ¼ cup vegetable oil
1½ pounds thinly sliced veal, cut into pieces
    4 slices salami, cut up
    1 medium onion, minced
    8 ounces sliced mushrooms
    2 green peppers, julienned
    1 teaspoon salt
    ¼ teaspoon pepper
    ¼ teaspoon oregano
    ¼ teaspoon garlic powder
    1 cup Marsala wine

Heat oil in a large frying pan. Add veal and sauté until browned. Add salami, onions, mushrooms, green peppers, salt, pepper, oregano and garlic powder. Sauté for five minutes. Add wine and simmer for ten minutes over low heat. Serves 4.

Baked Saltimbocca

    ½ cup grated Parmesan cheese
    ½ cup bread crumbs
    1 teaspoon salt
    ¼ teaspoon pepper
    ¼ teaspoon oregano
    ¼ teaspoon garlic powder
    ¼ teaspoon sage
    2 tablespoons vegetable oil
    2 tablespoons butter
    8 slices veal cutlets, pounded thin
    8 slices prosciutto ham
    8 slices mozzarella cheese
    1 cup warm water

Combine Parmesan cheese, bread crumbs, salt, pepper, oregano, garlic powder and sage in a small bowl. Coat veal with bread and cheese mixture. Heat oil and butter in a large frying pan and sauté veal for one minute on both sides. Place veal in a greased 9 x 12-inch pan and top with a slice of ham and a slice of mozzarella cheese. Bake at 375° for twenty-five minutes or until cheese is melted. Add warm water to skillet in which veal was cooked. Stir well. Pour over Saltimbocca and serve. Serves 4.

Ossobuco

    ¼ cup butter
    ½ cup vegetable oil
    4 veal shanks
    1 cup flour
    1 teaspoon salt
    ¼ teaspoon pepper
    ¼ teaspoon oregano
    ¼ teaspoon garlic powder
    ½ cup white Chablis wine
    1 29-ounce can tomato sauce
    2 tablespoons chopped parsley
    1 bay leaf
    1 teaspoon basil

Heat butter and oil in a large saucepan. Dredge veal in flour. Brown on all sides. Season with salt, pepper, oregano and garlic powder. Add wine. Reduce heat and cook for fifteen minutes. Add tomato sauce, parsley, bay leaf and basil. Simmer, covered, for two hours, stirring occasionally. Discard bay leaf. Serves 4.

Veal Sandwiches

       8 thin slices veal
       8 slices prosciutto ham
       8 slices mozzarella cheese
    1½ cups bread crumbs
       ¼ cup grated Romano cheese
       1 teaspoon salt
       ¼ teaspoon pepper
       ¼ teaspoon oregano
       ¼ teaspoon garlic powder
       3 eggs, lightly beaten
       ¼ cup vegetable oil
       2 tablespoons butter

Place veal on a flat surface. Place one slice of ham and one slice of cheese on each slice of veal. Fasten with toothpicks. Mix together bread crumbs, Romano cheese, salt, pepper, oregano and garlic powder. Dip each sandwich in egg, then in bread crumbs to coat both sides. Heat oil and butter in a large frying pan. Brown sandwiches on each side until golden. Place in a baking dish and bake at 375° for eight to ten minutes or until cheese is melted. Serves 4.

Lamb Stew with Peas

       ¼ cup vegetable oil
       2 tablespoons butter
    1½ pounds lamb stew meat
       2 medium onions, chopped
       2 cloves garlic, minced
       1 teaspoon mint flakes
    1¼ teaspoons salt
       ¼ teaspoon pepper
       ¼ teaspoon oregano
       1 17-ounce can peas, undrained

Heat oil and butter in a Dutch oven. Add meat and brown lightly. Add onions, garlic, mint, salt, pepper and oregano and simmer for twenty to thirty minutes or until meat is tender, stirring occasionally. Add peas and liquid. Cook for five to ten minutes over low heat. Serves 4.

Lamb with Italian Rice Pilaf

          Italian Rice Pilaf (recipe on page 41)
       4 loin lamb chops
       2 tablespoons lemon juice
       2 teaspoons oregano
          Salt to taste
       1 tomato, cut into four wedges
          Whole pitted ripe olives

Prepare Italian Rice Pilaf. Brush lamb chops with lemon juice and sprinkle with oregano. When Pilaf is done, broil lamb chops about four inches from heating element for eight to ten minutes on each side. Sprinkle with salt. Spoon Pilaf onto a serving platter. Surround with lamb chops. Garnish with tomato and olives. Serves 4.

Bracciole of Lamb

    1½ pounds lamb steak, thinly sliced
    1¼ teaspoons salt
       ¼ teaspoon pepper
       ¼ teaspoon oregano
       1 medium onion, thinly sliced
       2 cloves garlic, minced
       ¼ cup grated Romano cheese
       ¼ cup vegetable oil
       1 teaspoon rosemary
       ½ cup dry white wine

Flatten lamb steaks with a mallet and cut into four-inch pieces. Sprinkle lamb with salt, pepper and oregano. Place slices of onion, garlic and cheese in the center of each piece of lamb. Roll meat and fasten with toothpicks. Heat oil in a large frying pan. Brown lamb rolls over moderate heat until golden. Sprinkle with rosemary. Pour wine over all. Reduce heat. Cover and cook for twenty minutes or until meat is done. Serves 4.

Breast of Lamb Sicilian Style

       2 to 2½ pounds breast of lamb, fat trimmed
          Salt and pepper to taste
       1 cup bread crumbs
       1 tablespoon minced green onion
       1 tablespoon minced parsley
       1 clove garlic, minced
       ½ teaspoon oregano

Place lamb, meaty side down, in a large baking dish. Sprinkle with salt and pepper. Bake for thirty minutes at 450°. Turn and bake for fifteen minutes. Turn meat and drain fat. Combine remaining ingredients and mix well. With lamb meaty side up, sprinkle bread crumb mixture on top and bake for fifteen to twenty minutes, or until crumbs are nicely browned. Cut into serving pieces. Serves 4.

"Oregano should be used very sparingly because it is a bitter spice. Too much oregano can ruin a meal prepared by even the best cook."

Tony's Chicken

    2 small chickens, cut into small pieces
    1 teaspoon salt
    ¼ teaspoon pepper
    ¼ teaspoon oregano
    ¼ teaspoon garlic powder
    ¾ cup vegetable oil
    2 medium onions, chopped
    2 green peppers, chopped
    2 cups sliced mushrooms
    ½ cup Chablis wine

Toss chicken with salt, pepper, oregano, garlic powder and one-quarter cup oil. Place on baking sheet, skin side up. Bake at 375° for fifty to sixty minutes. Place baked chicken in a casserole. Heat remaining one-half cup oil in a frying pan and sauté onions, green peppers and mushrooms until onions are transparent. Spoon mushrooms and onions over chicken. Pour wine over all. Cover and bake at 350° for one hour. Serves 4 to 6.

Chicken Vesuvio

    1 2½- to 3-pound chicken
    4 potatoes, peeled and cut into pieces
    ¼ cup vegetable oil
    2 cloves garlic, minced
    1½ teaspoons salt
    ¼ teaspoon pepper
    ¼ teaspoon oregano
    ½ cup cooking sherry
    1 cup Chicken Broth (recipe below)

Toss chicken and potatoes with oil, garlic, salt, pepper and oregano. Place in a baking dish skin side up. Bake at 375° for one hour, or until chicken is tender. Remove from oven and place chicken in a large frying pan. Add sherry and Broth. Simmer for five minutes. Serves 4.

Chicken Broth

    Chicken neck and giblets
    1 quart water
    2 tablespoons minced parsley
    1 teaspoon salt
    ½ cup chopped onion
    1 rib celery, sliced

Place chicken parts in a two-quart saucepan. Add water. Bring to a boil; reduce heat and skim. Add parsley, salt, onion and celery. Cook over low heat for ninety minutes.

Grilled Chicken

    1 2½- to 3-pound chicken, cut in pieces
    1 teaspoon salt
    1 teaspoon rosemary
    1 teaspoon curry powder
    ¼ teaspoon oregano
    ¼ teaspoon paprika

Rub chicken with spices. Grill until chicken is golden brown. Serves 4.

Chicken Spread Italiano

    2 cups minced, cooked chicken
      Garlic powder and oregano to taste
    ½ cup diced celery
    ¼ cup chopped stuffed olives
    1 teaspoon mustard
    1 cup mayonnaise

Combine all ingredients and mix thoroughly. Chill well. Spread on bread or hamburger buns. Makes 6 sandwiches.

Chicken Cacciatore

    ¼ cup olive oil
    1 teaspoon salt
    ⅛ teaspoon pepper
    1 2½- to 3-pound chicken, cut into pieces
    1 clove garlic, minced
    2 medium onions, chopped
    12 mushrooms, sliced
    1 green pepper, cut into large cubes
    ½ cup sliced black olives
    1 8-ounce can tomato sauce
    ½ cup dry white or red wine
    1 cup hot chicken broth
    1 teaspoon basil
    ½ teaspoon dried mint
    ½ teaspoon oregano
    1 bay leaf
    1 pound pasta of your choice
      Grated Romano cheese

Heat oil in a large saucepan. Sprinkle salt and pepper over chicken. Brown on both sides in oil. Remove chicken from frying pan. Add garlic and onions and sauté until golden. Place mushrooms, green pepper and olives in a large baking dish. Arrange chicken on top of vegetables. Combine tomato sauce, wine, broth and herbs and pour over chicken. Bake at 350° for one hour, or until chicken is tender. Serves 4.

Chicken Livers

¼ cup vegetable oil
1 pound chicken livers
2 medium onions, chopped
2 cloves garlic, minced
1 teaspoon salt
¼ teaspoon pepper
¼ teaspoon oregano
½ teaspoon nutmeg
½ teaspoon cinnamon
4 tablespoons tomato sauce
¼ cup Chablis wine

Heat oil in a medium saucepan. Add livers, onions and garlic. Sauté until onions are transparent. Add salt, pepper, oregano, nutmeg and cinnamon. Stir in tomato sauce. Add wine and cook until liver is done. Serves 4.

Peasant-Style Chicken

1 2½- to 3-pound chicken, cut up
¼ cup vegetable oil
6 potatoes, peeled and quartered
2 medium onions, chopped
2 tomatoes, chopped
1 cup white wine
1 teaspoon salt
¼ teaspoon pepper
¼ teaspoon oregano
¼ teaspoon garlic powder

Place chicken in a large bowl. Add remaining ingredients and toss lightly. Place all in a roasting pan and bake at 375° for seventy-five minutes or until chicken is done. Serves 4.

Chicken Stew

1 tablespoon vegetable oil
¼ pound butter
4 ribs celery, cut into pieces
2 teaspoons chopped parsley
½ pound mushrooms, sliced
2 cloves garlic, minced
2 small onions, chopped
2 carrots, chopped
1 medium fryer, cut into serving pieces
1 6-ounce can tomato paste
1 6-ounce can water
1 teaspoon salt
¼ teaspoon pepper
¼ teaspoon oregano
¼ teaspoon garlic powder

Heat oil and butter in a Dutch oven. Add celery, parsley, mushrooms, garlic, onions and carrots. Sauté until onions are transparent. Add chicken and brown on all sides. Add tomato paste and

water. Season with salt, pepper, oregano and garlic powder. Cover and simmer over low heat for forty-five minutes or until chicken is tender. If sauce is too thick, add more water. Serves 4.

Chicken Kiev Italian Style

2 whole chicken breasts, boned and halved
2 eggs, lightly beaten
1 cup bread crumbs
¼ cup grated Romano cheese
1 teaspoon salt
¼ teaspoon pepper
¼ teaspoon oregano
¼ teaspoon garlic powder

Flatten chicken breasts with a mallet to one-quarter-inch thickness. Place a ball of chilled Garlic Butter in the center of each chicken breast. Roll up chicken, making sure butter is completely enclosed. Secure with toothpicks. Combine bread crumbs, cheese, salt, pepper, oregano and garlic powder. Dip chicken in eggs and then coat with bread crumb mixture. Chill chicken for one hour. Bake at 375° for one hour or fry in hot oil until golden brown. Serves 4.

Garlic Butter

1 stick butter, softened
¼ cup grated Romano cheese
1 tablespoon minced parsley
2 cloves garlic, minced
1 teaspoon salt
¼ teaspoon pepper
¼ teaspoon oregano

Thoroughly combine all ingredients. Form butter into four balls. Chill thoroughly.

Chicken Parmesan

1 2½- to 3-pound chicken, cut into pieces
2 cups bread crumbs
½ cup grated Parmesan cheese
1 teaspoon salt
¼ teaspoon pepper
2 cloves garlic, minced
¼ teaspoon oregano
2 eggs, lightly beaten
⅔ cup vegetable oil

Combine bread crumbs, cheese, salt, pepper, garlic and oregano. Dip chicken in eggs and then in bread crumb mixture. Heat oil in a large frying pan and fry each piece on both sides until browned. Remove from pan. Place on baking sheet and bake at 350° for one hour. Serves 4.

Breast of Chicken

- ¼ cup vegetable oil
- ¼ cup butter
- 4 large mushrooms, sliced
- 1 clove garlic, minced
- 1½ teaspoons salt
- ¼ teaspoon pepper
- ¼ teaspoon oregano
- 4 slices mozzarella cheese
- 4 slices prosciutto ham
- 1 cup chicken broth
- ½ cup Chablis wine
- 4 whole chicken breasts, boned, skinned and flattened

Heat oil and butter in a large frying pan. Add mushrooms and garlic and sauté for four minutes. Add salt, pepper and oregano. Lay chicken flat in a large baking dish. Place a slice of mozzarella cheese and a slice of prosciutto on each. Spoon mushroom mixture over top. Pour chicken broth and wine into frying pan. Simmer for five minutes. Pour over chicken breasts. Bake at 375° for thirty minutes. Serves 4.

Chicken Vignieri

- 2 whole chicken breasts, halved, boned and flattened
- ¼ cup butter, melted
- 1½ cups bread crumbs
- ½ cup grated Romano cheese
- 1½ teaspoons salt
- ¼ teaspoon pepper
- ¼ teaspoon oregano
- ¼ teaspoon garlic powder
- 4 slices ham
- 4 slices Provolone cheese
- ¼ cup vegetable oil
- 1 cup sliced mushrooms
- ½ cup Chablis wine
- ½ cup water

Dip chicken breasts in butter. Combine bread crumbs, Romano cheese, salt, pepper, oregano and garlic powder. Coat chicken with bread crumb mixture. Lay chicken breasts flat. Place a slice of ham and a slice of cheese on each and roll up. Heat oil in a large frying pan. Sauté chicken on both sides until golden brown. Add mushrooms and sauté over low heat for ten minutes. Pour wine over all. Sauté for five minutes. Add water. Reduce heat, cover and cook for fifteen minutes. Serves 4.

Mediterranean Style Chicken

- 1 2½- to 3-pound roasting chicken
- 2 tablespoons butter, softened
- 2 tablespoons olive oil
- 2 tablespoons lemon juice
- 1 teaspoon oregano
  Salt and pepper to taste
- 4 potatoes, peeled and halved

Brush chicken with butter. In a small bowl, beat together oil, lemon juice, oregano, salt and pepper. Brush chicken inside and out with above mixture. Place in a shallow baking pan. Bake at 400° for about one hour or until tender. Baste chicken with juices after fifteen minutes of baking time. Arrange potatoes in baking pan thirty minutes prior to end of baking time. Serves 4.

Chicken with Spaghetti

- ¼ pound butter, melted
- ½ cup parsley sprigs
- 2 cloves garlic, halved
  Salt and pepper to taste
- 1 teaspoon basil
- ½ teaspoon oregano
- 2 tablespoons vegetable oil
- 1 tablespoon lemon juice
- 1 2½- to 3-pound chicken, cut into pieces
- ½ pound spaghetti
  Parsley sprigs to garnish

Place butter, parsley, garlic, salt, pepper, basil and oregano in an electric blender. Cover; blend at high speed until parsley is finely chopped. Set aside three tablespoons of the herb mixture for the chicken. Use the remainder to toss with spaghetti. Beat together oil and lemon juice with a fork. Brush chicken with mixture. Sprinkle with salt and pepper. Broil chicken about eight inches from heating element for about forty-five minutes, or until golden. Turn chicken after twenty minutes of broiling. Brush each side with reserved herb mixture during the last four minutes of broiling. About fifteen minutes before chicken is done, prepare spaghetti and drain. Toss with reserved three tablespoons herb mixture. Arrange chicken around edge of platter. Garnish with parsley sprigs. Serves 4 to 6.

Main Dishes/Seafood

White Fish

- 1 large white fish, cleaned
- 3 carrots, cut into small pieces
- 3 potatoes, peeled and cut into small pieces
- 2 cloves garlic, minced
- 2 medium onions, chopped
- 2 teaspoons chopped parsley
- 1 bay leaf
- 5 cups water
- 1½ teaspoons salt
- ¼ teaspoon pepper
- ¼ cup butter
- 1 tablespoon vegetable oil

Place all ingredients, except butter and oil, in a deep pan. Bring to a boil and cook for twenty to twenty-five minutes, or until fish is tender. Place fish on a large serving platter. Arrange vegetables around fish. Heat butter and oil and pour over fish. Serves 2 to 4.

Shrimp Fritters

- 1 6½-ounce can shrimp, chopped
- 2 cups flour
- ½ cup grated Romano cheese
- 2 cloves garlic, minced
- ¼ cup onions, minced
- ¼ cup green pepper, minced
- ¼ cup celery, minced
- 1 teaspoon salt
- ¼ teaspoon pepper
- ¼ teaspoon oregano
- 2 cups vegetable oil

Mix all ingredients except oil, in a large bowl. Add enough water to make a mixture the consistency of pancake batter. Heat oil in a large frying pan. Drop batter by tablespoonsful into oil. Fry on both sides until golden brown. Serves 4.

Neopolitan Snails

- 2 pounds snails in shells
- ½ cup vegetable oil
- 2 medium onions, chopped
- 2 cloves garlic, minced
- 4 tablespoons tomato paste
- 3 cups hot water
- 1 teaspoon salt
- ¼ teaspoon pepper
- ¼ teaspoon oregano
- 2 teaspoons chopped parsley

Scrub snails with a stiff brush. Rinse thoroughly. Place in a large bowl of salted water, cover and soak for one-half hour. Pour oil in a deep kettle. Add onions and garlic and sauté until onions are transparent. Stir in tomato paste. Cook over moderate heat for seven minutes, stirring often. Stir in water. Drain snails and place in kettle. Cook over moderate heat for ten minutes. Add salt, pepper, oregano and parsley. Cover and simmer for twenty-five minutes, stirring occasionally. Serve in soup bowls. Remove snails from shells with oyster forks. Serves 4.

Steamed Clams

- 24 fresh clams
- 3 tablespoons vegetable oil
- 3 cloves garlic, minced
- ½ cup water
- 1¼ teaspoons salt
- ¼ teaspoon pepper
- ¼ teaspoon oregano
- 3 tablespoons chopped parsley
- 1 lemon, cut in wedges

Wash and rinse clams thoroughly. Place oil and garlic in a large saucepan. Sauté for four minutes. Add clams, water, salt, pepper, oregano and parsley. Cover and steam over moderate heat for fifteen minutes, or until clams open. Place clams on serving platter. Garnish with lemon wedges. Serves 4.

Lobster with Tomato Sauce

- 2 large lobster tails
- 2 tablespoons vegetable oil
- 2 tablespoons butter
- 1 small onion, chopped
- 2 cloves garlic, minced
- 1 teaspoon salt
- ¼ teaspoon pepper
- ¼ teaspoon oregano
- ½ teaspoon basil
- 1 29-ounce can tomato sauce
- 1 pound pasta of your choice
- ½ cup grated Romano cheese

Boil lobster until done. Cool. Remove meat from shell by splitting lengthwise. Cut meat into large pieces. Heat oil and butter in a medium-size saucepan. Add onions, garlic, salt, pepper, oregano, basil and tomato sauce. Cook for thirty minutes over low heat, stirring occasionally. Add lobster and cook for forty-five minutes over low heat, stirring occasionally. Prepare pasta according to package directions and drain. Place pasta in a serving bowl and spoon on lobster sauce. Sprinkle Romano cheese on top. Serves 4.

Codfish with Raisins and Pine Nuts

¼ cup vegetable oil
2 tablespoons butter
2 medium onions, minced
2 cloves garlic, minced
2½ cups Italian plum tomatoes, crushed
12 black olives
1 rib celery, cut and sliced
½ teaspoon basil
1 teaspoon salt
¼ teaspoon pepper
¼ teaspoon oregano
2 tablespoons raisins
¼ cup pine nuts
1½ pounds codfish filets, cut in pieces

Heat oil and butter in a large saucepan. Add onions and garlic and sauté until onions are transparent. Add tomatoes, olives, celery, basil, salt, pepper, oregano, raisins and nuts. Simmer for fifteen minutes over low heat. Add codfish and cook for forty minutes. Serves 4 to 6.

Scampi alla Lombardo

4 tablespoons butter
24 shrimp, cleaned and deveined
2 cloves garlic, minced
2 teaspoons chopped parsley
1 small onion, chopped
1 teaspoon salt
¼ teaspoon pepper
¼ teaspoon oregano
1 bay leaf
¼ teaspoon fennel powder
½ cup white Chablis wine

Heat butter in a large saucepan. Add shrimp, garlic, parsley and onions. Sauté for five minutes. Add salt, pepper, oregano, bay leaf and fennel powder. Stir in wine and simmer for fifteen to twenty minutes. Serves 4.

Casserole of Scallops

¼ cup vegetable oil
2 tablespoons butter
1½ pounds scallops
1 medium onion, chopped
1 green pepper, chopped
1 cup sliced mushrooms
1 29-ounce can tomato sauce
1 teaspoon salt
¼ teaspoon pepper
¼ teaspoon oregano
½ cup white wine
½ teaspoon basil
3 cups cooked rice
½ cup grated Romano cheese

Heat oil and butter in a medium-size frying pan. Sauté scallops, turning frequently, about five to seven minutes. Remove scallops and set aside. In the same frying pan add onions, green pepper and mushrooms. Cook for a few minutes longer, stirring often. Add remaining ingredients, except rice, cheese and scallops. Bring to a boil and add scallops. Reduce heat and cook for ten to fifteen minutes, stirring occasionally. Place rice in a four- to five-quart casserole. Pour sauce over rice and sprinkle on cheese. Bake at 375° for twenty to twenty-five minutes. Serves 4.

Spaghetti con Tuna

¼ cup vegetable oil
1 medium onion, chopped
3 cloves garlic, minced
1 teaspoon chopped parsley
1 6½-ounce can tuna fish, drained and flaked
10 pitted black olives, sliced
2 cups tomato sauce
1 teaspoon salt
¼ teaspoon pepper
¼ teaspoon oregano
1 pound spaghetti
Grated Parmesan cheese

Heat oil in a large saucepan. Sauté onions, garlic and parsley for three minutes. Add tuna, olives and tomato sauce. Season with salt, pepper and oregano. Simmer slowly for forty-five minutes. Cook spaghetti according to package directions. Drain. Spoon tuna mixture over spaghetti. Sprinkle Parmesan cheese over all. Serves 4 to 6.

Cioppino

¼ cup olive oil
½ cup chopped green pepper
½ cup chopped onion
2 medium cloves garlic, minced
¼ teaspoon oregano
1 29-ounce can tomato sauce
1 cup water
½ cup dry white wine
1 pound shrimp, shelled and deveined
2 lobster tails, cooked, shelled and cut into pieces
2 tablespoons chopped parsley
1 bay leaf
1 pound haddock filets, cut into 2-inch pieces

Heat oil in a large frying pan. Add green pepper, onions, garlic and oregano and sauté until onions are transparent. Add remaining ingredients, except haddock. Simmer over low heat for ten minutes. Add haddock and cook for ten additional minutes, stirring occasionally. Serves 4 to 6.

Tuna with Rice

- 1 cup raw rice
- 1 6½-ounce can tuna fish, drained and flaked
- 1 teaspoon salt
- ¼ teaspoon pepper
- ¼ teaspoon oregano
- ¼ teaspoon garlic powder
- ¼ cup butter
- ¼ cup grated Romano cheese

Prepare rice according to package directions. In a large saucepan, over low heat, combine rice, tuna fish, salt, pepper, oregano and garlic powder. Stir in butter and cheese. Serves 4.

Filets of Sole with Wine

- ¼ cup vegetable oil
- 2 tablespoons butter
- 1 medium onion, chopped
- 2 cloves garlic, minced
- 1 teaspoon salt
- ¼ teaspoon pepper
- 2 teaspoons chopped parsley
- ¼ teaspoon oregano
- ½ pound mushrooms, sliced
- 1 tablespoon tomato sauce
- ¼ cup Vermouth or any red wine
- 4 filets of sole

Heat oil and butter in a large frying pan. Add onions and garlic and sauté until onions are transparent. Add salt, pepper, parsley, oregano, mushrooms, tomato sauce and wine. Simmer for five to seven minutes. Place fish in a baking pan. Pour on wine mixture. Bake at 375° for ten to twelve minutes, or until fish is tender. Serves 4.

Squid with Spaghetti

- 1½ pounds squid
- ½ cup vegetable oil
- 2 medium onions, chopped
- 2 cloves garlic, minced
- 1 29-ounce can tomato sauce
- 1 teaspoon salt
- ¼ teaspoon pepper
- 1 bay leaf
- ¼ teaspoon oregano
- 1 pound spaghetti, prepared according to package directions and drained
- ¾ cup grated Romano cheese

Clean squid by removing skin, tentacles and ink sac from body. Wash thoroughly. Cut into one-half-inch rings. Heat oil in a large saucepan. Add onions and garlic and sauté until onions are transparent. Add squid and sauté for five minutes. Add tomato sauce, pepper, bay leaf and oregano. Reduce heat and cook for about two hours, stirring occasionally. Place cooked spaghetti on a serving platter. Sprinkle on Romano cheese. Spoon squid sauce over all. Serves 4 to 6.

Mussels with Rice

- 2 dozen mussels
- 1 tablespoon salt
- ⅔ cup water
- ⅔ cup vegetable oil
- 2 medium onions, minced
- 2 cloves garlic, minced
- 2 teaspoons tomato paste
- 1 teaspoon salt
- ¼ teaspoon pepper
- ¼ teaspoon oregano
- 3 cups boiling water
- 1½ cups raw rice
- ½ cup grated Romano cheese

Place mussels and one tablespoon salt in a large saucepan; cover with cold water. Soak for twenty minutes. Scrape outside of shells until clean. Rinse. Heat oil in a large frying pan. Add onions and garlic and sauté until onions are transparent. Add tomato paste, salt, pepper and oregano. Cover and cook until mussels open. Add water and rice; Stir. Cover and cook until rice is done. Add cheese and serve. Serves 4.

Fried Frog Legs

- 12 frog legs
- ⅔ cup Chablis wine
- 1 teaspoon salt
- ¼ teaspoon pepper
- ¼ teaspoon oregano
- ¼ teaspoon garlic powder
- 1 small onion, chopped
- ½ teaspoon nutmeg
- 2 eggs, lightly beaten
- 1¼ cups flour
- 1¼ cups vegetable oil
- ¼ cup grated Romano cheese

Rinse frog legs under water and pat dry. Combine wine, salt, pepper, oregano, garlic powder, onions and nutmeg in a medium-size bowl. Add frog legs and marinate for forty-five minutes. Dip frog legs in egg, then dredge in flour. Heat oil in a large frying pan. Fry legs on all sides until tender and golden brown. When tender, sprinkle with cheese. Serves 4.

Shrimp with Italian Rice Pilaf

1½ tablespoons butter
1 medium onion, minced
1 carrot, peeled and slivered
¼ cup white wine
1 pound shrimp, cleaned and deveined
1 teaspoon salt
¼ teaspoon pepper
¼ teaspoon oregano
2 tablespoons tomato sauce

Heat butter in a large frying pan. Add onions and carrots and sauté until onions are transparent. Add wine; cook until wine is evaporated. Add shrimp and sauté for three or four minutes. Add salt, pepper, oregano and tomato sauce. Simmer for five minutes, stirring often. Spoon over Italian Rice Pilaf (recipe on page 41.) Serves 4.

Italian Tuna Pie

6 eggs
½ cup milk
1 6½-ounce tuna fish, drained and flaked
½ cup grated mozzarella cheese
½ cup grated Romano cheese
1 teaspoon salt
¼ teaspoon oregano
¼ teaspoon pepper
¼ teaspoon garlic powder
¼ teaspoon basil
1 unbaked 9-inch pastry shell

Beat eggs with milk in a medium-size mixing bowl. Add remaining ingredients and spoon into pastry shell. Bake at 375° until a knife inserted in the center comes out clean. Serves 4 to 6.

Grilled Sun Fish

8 small sun fish, cleaned
Flour
Salt, pepper, oregano and garlic
powder to taste
Lemon wedges

Wash fish in salted water. Open cavities and flour all sides. Season with salt, pepper, oregano and garlic powder. Grill until all sides are cooked. Serve with lemon wedges. Serves 4.

Shrimp Scampi

4 tablespoons butter
2 tablespoons vegetable oil
1 pound shrimp, deveined,
   boiled until pink and drained
1½ cups sliced mushrooms
1 teaspoon salt
¼ teaspoon pepper
¼ teaspoon oregano
1 tablespoon chopped parsley
¼ teaspoon garlic powder
¼ cup white wine

Heat butter and oil in a large frying pan. Add shrimp, mushrooms, salt, pepper, oregano, parsley and garlic. Simmer for five minutes over moderate heat. Add wine and simmer an additional five minutes. Serve with Garlic Toast. Serves 4.

Garlic Toast

1 loaf French bread, halved lengthwise and
   sliced into 5-inch pieces
   Melted butter
   Garlic powder
   Romano or Parmesan cheese, optional

Brush butter on bread. Sprinkle garlic powder on each slice. Arrange bread on a baking sheet and broil until golden brown. For variety, sprinkle grated Romano or Parmesan cheese on each slice of bread before broiling. Serves 4 to 6.

Stuffed Squid

1½ pounds squid, cleaned
2 cups bread crumbs
¾ cup grated Romano cheese
2 eggs
1 teaspoon salt
¼ teaspoon pepper
½ teaspoon oregano
2 cloves garlic, minced
1½ cups tomato sauce
¼ cup white wine

Remove tentacles, ink sac and skin from squid. Cut tentacles in small pieces. In a small bowl, mix together bread crumbs, one-half cup Romano cheese, eggs, salt, pepper, oregano, garlic and tentacles. Fill squid with bread crumb mixture and place in a baking pan. Pour tomato sauce over all. Sprinkle with remaining Romano cheese. Pour wine over all and season with salt, pepper and oregano to taste. Bake at 350° for one hour. Serves 4.

Eggs and Rice

Eggs Florentine

¼ cup vegetable oil
1 pound fresh spinach, washed, dried and torn into pieces
1½ teaspoons salt
¼ teaspoon pepper
¼ cup grated Romano cheese
4 eggs
Vegetable oil

Heat oil in a large saucepan. Add spinach. Cover and cook for 10 minutes. Add salt, pepper and cheese. Place spinach in four individual baking dishes. Break one egg over each. Drizzle each with a small amount of oil. Bake at 350° until the eggs are cooked. Serves 4.

Shrimp and Egg Futula

¼ cup vegetable oil
2 tablespoons butter
1 pound shrimp, canned or fresh, shelled, deveined and washed
1 teaspoon salt
¼ teaspoon pepper
¼ teaspoon oregano
8 eggs, well-beaten
¼ cup grated Romano cheese

Heat oil and butter in a large frying pan. Add shrimp; season with salt, pepper and oregano. Stir in eggs and cheese. Cook over moderate heat until cheese is melted. Serves 4.

Artichoke Frittata

1 10-ounce package frozen artichoke hearts, thawed
1 tablespoon lemon juice
2 tablespoons vegetable oil
2 tablespoons butter
1 cup flour
6 eggs
3 tablespoons water
1 teaspoon salt
¼ teaspoon pepper
¼ teaspoon oregano
¼ teaspoon garlic powder
½ cup grated Romano cheese

Cut artichoke hearts in half lengthwise. Sprinkle with lemon juice. Heat oil and butter in a large frying pan. Dredge artichoke hearts in flour and brown on each side until golden. Remove and place in a greased two-quart casserole. Lightly beat eggs and water together. Combine salt, pepper, oregano, garlic and cheese. Add to eggs and mix well. Pour eggs over artichoke hearts and bake at 350° until knife inserted in center comes out clean. Serves 4.

Eggs alla Cacciatore

8 chicken livers, cut in halves
1 teaspoon salt
¼ teaspoon pepper
¼ teaspoon oregano
¼ cup vegetable oil
1 small onion, minced
1 green pepper, chopped
1 clove garlic, minced
2 tablespoons warm water
2 tablespoons tomato paste
¼ cup white wine
4 eggs

Season liver with salt, pepper and oregano. Heat oil in a small frying pan. Sauté liver, onions, green pepper and garlic until onions are transparent. Blend water with tomato paste. Add tomato paste mixture and wine. Cook for five minutes, stirring constantly. Drop in one egg at a time, trying not to break yolks. Cover pan and cook over low heat for five minutes. Serve hot on toasted English muffins. Serves 4.

Ham Frittata

¼ cup vegetable oil
2 medium onions, chopped
1 green pepper, minced
2 cloves garlic, minced
8 slices ham, diced
8 mushrooms, thinly sliced
8 eggs
1 teaspoon salt
¼ teaspoon pepper
¼ teaspoon oregano
¼ cup grated Parmesan cheese

Heat oil in a large frying pan. Add onions, peppers, garlic, ham and mushrooms and sauté until onions are transparent. Place eggs, salt, pepper and oregano in a bowl. Beat well. Add sautéed ingredients and mix lightly. Add cheese and mix lightly. Place in a greased square or oblong pan. Bake at 375° for forty-five minutes or until a knife inserted in center comes out clean. Serves 4 to 6.

Duaynes (Italian Rice Pilaf)

¼ cup vegetable oil
1 tablespoon butter
1½ cups cooked rice
1 large onion, chopped
1 cup cooked sliced mushrooms or
   1 8-ounce can
¼ cup grated Romano cheese
½ cup chicken broth
1 teaspoon salt
¼ teaspoon pepper
¼ teaspoon oregano
¼ teaspoon garlic powder

Heat oil and butter in a medium-size saucepan. Add onion and mushrooms and sauté until onions are transparent. Add remaining ingredients and mix well. Heat thoroughly. Serves 4.

Italian Fried Rice with Bacon

2 cups raw rice
1 tablespoon vegetable oil
2 tablespoons butter
6 slices bacon, cut into pieces
2 medium onions, minced
½ cup grated Romano cheese
1 teaspoon salt
¼ teaspoon pepper
¼ teaspoon oregano
¼ teaspoon garlic powder
2 eggs

Prepare rice according to package directions. Heat oil and butter in a large frying pan. Add bacon and sauté until crisp. Add onions and sauté until onions are transparent. Add rice, cheese, salt, pepper, oregano and garlic powder. Mix thoroughly. Add eggs, one at a time, stirring after each addition. Cook until eggs have thickened. Cover and simmer for five minutes over low heat. Serves 4.

Risotto Genoaese

1 stick butter
2 carrots, diced
2 medium onions, minced
3 ribs celery, chopped
½ pound ground veal
1 teaspoon salt
¼ teaspoon pepper
¼ teaspoon oregano
¼ teaspoon garlic powder
2 teaspoons chopped parsley
¼ teaspoon nutmeg
½ cup Chablis wine
2½ cups raw rice
2 tablespoons butter

Melt butter in a medium-size saucepan and sauté all vegetables until slightly tender. Stir in veal and cook until browned. Add salt, pepper, oregano, garlic, parsley and nutmeg. Stir in wine. Cover. Reduce heat and simmer for thirty-five minutes. Prepare rice according to package directions. Place in a large saucepan and add the two tablespoons butter. Pour on sauce and mix thoroughly. Serves 4.

Chicken Livers Risotto Veneziana

¼ pound chicken livers, cut in halves
2 medium onions, chopped
3 cloves garlic, minced
2 cups sliced mushrooms
3 tablespoons vegetable oil
3 tablespoons butter
¼ cup white wine
1 teaspoon salt
¼ teaspoon pepper
¼ teaspoon oregano
4 cups hot chicken broth
2 cups raw rice
¼ cup grated Romano cheese
2 tablespoons parsley

Sauté chicken livers, onions, garlic and mushrooms in oil and butter until tender. Simmer for five minutes. Add wine and season with salt, pepper and oregano. Bring chicken soup to a boil. Add rice, reduce heat and cover. Simmer for 20 minutes until rice is tender. Add cheese and parsley. Serve chicken livers over rice. Serves 6.

Oven Rice

1½ cups raw rice
1 teaspoon salt
¼ teaspoon pepper
¼ teaspoon oregano
1 small onion, chopped
2 cloves garlic, minced
4 tablespoons butter
4 cups boiling water
½ cup grated Romano cheese

Place rice, salt, pepper and oregano in a two-quart covered casserole. Mix in garlic and onions. Dot top with butter. Pour hot water over all. Sprinkle with Romano cheese. Cover and bake at 350° for forty-five minutes. When done, fluff rice with a fork. Serves 4 to 6.

Pasta

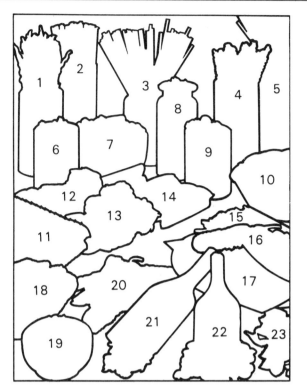

1 margherita 2 menucci 3 linguine (small tongues) 4 fusilli (twists) 5 vermicelli (little worms) 6 rotini 7 rigatoni 8 mostaccioli (mustaches) 9 gnocchi 10 conchiglioni (jumbo conch shells) 11 curly lasagna 12 lasagnette 13 fettucini (ribbons) 14 manicotti (sleeves) 15 macaroncelli (ziti or long macaroni) 16 spinach (fettucine 17 spinach egg lasagne 18 torroncini 19 ditalini 20 tagliatelle 21 orzo 22 elbow macaroni 23 cravatinne (bows) Not shown: farfalla (butterflies)

About Pasta

There are three basic varieties of pasta: domestic, imported and homemade, each with its own unique qualities.

Cooked domestic pasta tends to be gummier than imported Italian, so to avoid stickiness, do not overcook the pasta. Remember, the passwords in Italian are "al dente," or firm to the tooth. But for unrivaled texture and taste, the true gourmand will tell you that the best pasta is always homemade.

For each pound of pasta bring at least four quarts of water and one tablespoon salt to a rolling boil. Gradually add pasta and stir to separate the strands. Cooking times on the packages are usually too long, so begin checking for doneness before the cooking time is up. Pasta that is underdone has a hard core; overcooked pasta is mushy. Homemade pasta cooks more rapidly, so begin checking for doneness after the first minute.

Serving Pasta

Drain cooked pasta in a colander. Transfer to a heated bowl and stir in sauce. Serving size may vary, but generally speaking, one pound serves four as a main course, six as a first course.

Which Sauce to Serve

While there are really no rules to follow when deciding which pasta to use, here is a general suggestion—choose pasta with an intricate shape or one that has a hole in it, such as torroncini, rotini and ditalini, for thick sauces that contain meat and chunky vegetables. Thinner sauces are more compatible with spaghetti, vermicelli and the like.

Homemade pastas differ from commercial in that they tend to absorb sauces more readily.

Homemade Pasta

Homemade pasta can be rolled out by hand or through a pasta machine. To roll by hand, divide the dough into thirds. Work with one-third at a time, covering remaining portions with a towel. On a floured board or pastry cloth, roll out dough as thinly as possible. Cover and let rest for ten minutes.

To roll out dough with a pasta machine, divide dough in half and feed through rollers set on the widest opening. Fold dough and roll again through the next narrowest opening. Repeat this procedure until dough has gone through the narrowest opening. Finally, run dough through the cutters and allow to dry for at least one hour before using.

Storing Pasta

Cut pasta and spread out to dry completely. Wrap in clear plastic or foil and place in an airtight container. Store in a cool, dry place until ready to use. To freeze pasta, cut and allow to dry for at least one hour. Seal in moistureproof wrap.

To store stuffed pasta, first fill and shape. Dust lightly with flour and allow to dry for one hour. Stuffed pasta can be kept for up to three days by refrigerating in a covered container.

As with unstuffed pasta, stuffed pasta may also be frozen by sealing in moistureproof wrap.

Both stuffed and unstuffed pasta may be frozen for up to eight months.

Pasta

"Cooking times on the packages are usually a little long, so begin checking for doneness before the cooking time is up."

Basic Pasta Dough

2½ cups flour
3 eggs
1 teaspoon salt
2 tablespoons shortening
3 tablespoons water

Place flour in a large bowl. Make a well in the center. Add remaining ingredients and mix well to make a stiff dough. Add more flour or water if necessary. Work dough with the heel of your hand on a lightly floured board, always pushing away from you. Cover and let dough rest for fifteen minutes. Roll out dough on a floured board or use a pasta machine. Yields about 1 pound pasta.

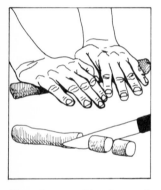 

To make gnocchi, roll a small amount of dough into a rope one inch in diameter. Cut into one-inch lengths.

Flour each piece lightly and roll firmly with your thumb on the fine side of a lightly floured grater to form a shell.

Ricotta Cheese Gnocchi

1½ cups ricotta cheese
2 tablespoons vegetable oil
2 eggs
½ cup grated Romano cheese
1 teaspoon salt
¼ teaspoon pepper
¼ teaspoon oregano
¼ teaspoon garlic powder
3 cups flour

Combine all ingredients, except flour; mix well. Add flour a little at a time and mix well to form a stiff dough. Add more flour if necessary. Break off pieces of dough and roll into ropes three-fourths inch in diameter. Cut into one-inch pieces. Roll each piece of dough on the fine side of a lightly-floured grater to form shells. Fill a six-quart kettle two-thirds full of water and bring to a rolling boil. Add gnocchi. When gnocchi surfaces, cook for five to seven minutes, or until al dente. Serve with your favorite sauce. Serves 4 to 6.

Spinach Gnocchi

2 cups ricotta cheese
½ pound fresh spinach, cooked, drained and pureed
2 eggs
½ cup grated Romano cheese
2 tablespoons shortening
1 teaspoon salt
¼ teaspoon pepper
¼ teaspoon oregano
¼ teaspoon garlic powder
3 cups flour

Combine all ingredients, except flour, in a large bowl. Slowly add flour and mix by hand until well-blended. If necessary, add more flour to make a stiff dough. Roll a small amount of dough at a time to form ropes one inch in diameter. Cut into one-inch lengths, flour lightly and roll each piece firmly with thumb on the fine side of a floured grater to form a shell. Bring salted water to a boil in a six- to eight-quart pan. Add gnocchi a few at a time. When gnocchi rises to surface, remove with a slotted spoon. Serve with a favorite sauce. Serve 4 to 6.

Ravioli with Raisin Filling

3 cups flour
3 tablespoons water
3 eggs, lightly beaten
1 tablespoon vegetable oil, plus
2 tablespoons shortening
1 tablespoon salt

Place flour in a large bowl. Form a well in the center. Drop in eggs. Add oil, shortening and salt. Mix thoroughly, adding water a little at a time. Turn out onto a lightly floured board and knead until dough is smooth and elastic, about eight minutes. Cover dough and let rest for five minutes. Divide dough into five sections and roll out into very thin rectangles. Cut rectangles into 3 x 10-inch strips. Drop Raisin Filling (recipe on page 53) by teaspoonsful on each strip at two-inch intervals. Place another strip of dough on top. Press lightly to mold top to bottom dough. Cut into two-inch squares with a knife. Seal edges with fork tines. Cook ravioli in boiling salted water until tender and drain. Serve with a favorite sauce. Sprinkle with Parmesan cheese. Serves 6.

Cannelloni

- 2 cups flour
- 1 teaspoon salt
- 2 eggs
- ½ cup water
- 2 tablespoons vegetable oil

Combine flour and salt in a large bowl. Add eggs, water and oil. Mix thoroughly. Place on a floured board and knead to the consistency of pie dough. Add more flour or water, if necessary. Cover dough and let rest for ten minutes. Divide dough in half and roll out into two rectangles. Cut rectangles into five-inch squares. Bring four quarts of water to a rolling boil. Drop in squares and cook for about six minutes. Drain. Rinse in cold water and drain again. Fill with desired filling, roll up and place in a lightly greased baking dish. Pour on two cups tomato sauce and one cup Bechamel Sauce (recipe on page 52). Bake at 375° for forty minutes. Serves 4.

Baked Rigatoni with Ricotta

- 1 pound rigatoni
- 3 cups ricotta cheese
  Salt, pepper, oregano and garlic powder to taste
- ½ pound prosciutto ham, cut into cubes
- ½ cup grated Romano cheese
  Bechamel Sauce (recipe on page 52)

Prepare rigatoni according to package directions and drain. Using a greased 2½-quart casserole, layer rigatoni, ricotta cheese, seasonings and ham, ending with pasta. Sprinkle on Romano cheese. Pour Bechamel Sauce over all. Bake at 375° for forty-five minutes. Serves 4 to 6.

Linguine with Mixed Vegetables

- 2 tablespoons vegetable oil
- 2 tablespoons butter
- 2 medium onions, chopped
- 2 cloves garlic, minced
- 1 small eggplant, peeled and cubed
- 3 small carrots, peeled and chopped
- 3½ cups Italian plum tomatoes, pureed
- 1 teaspoon salt
- 2 basil leaves
- ¼ cup pine nuts
- 1 pound linguine
- ½ cup grated Romano cheese

Heat oil and butter in a large frying pan. Add onions, garlic and eggplant and sauté until onions are transparent. Add carrots, tomatoes, salt and basil. Simmer slowly for ninety minutes.

Add pine nuts. Prepare linguini according to package directions and drain. Stir in sauce and cheese. Serves 4 to 6.

Ditalini and Potatoes

- ¼ cup vegetable oil
- 4 large potatoes, peeled and cubed
- 2 onions, chopped
- 2 cloves garlic, minced
- 1 15-ounce can tomato sauce
- 1 teaspoon salt
- ¼ teaspoon pepper
- ¼ teaspoon oregano
- 2 teaspoons basil
- 2 teaspoons chopped parsley
- 1 pound ditalini (small tubes)
- ½ cup grated Romano cheese

Heat oil in a large saucepan. Add potatoes, onions and garlic and sauté for ten to twelve minutes. Add tomato sauce, salt, pepper, oregano, basil and parsley. Cook over low heat for forty-five minutes, stirring occasionally. Prepare ditalini according to package directions and drain. Mix ditalini with potato mixture and cheese. Serves 4.

Spaghetti alla Casserole

- ¼ cup vegetable oil
- 2 tablespoons butter
- 2 medium onions, chopped
- 2 cloves garlic, minced
- 1 cup sliced mushrooms
- 1½ teaspoons salt
- ¼ teaspoon pepper
- 1¼ teaspoons oregano
- 2½ cups Italian plum tomatoes
- 1 teaspoon basil
- 1 pound Italian sausage, cut into 1-inch pieces and baked until done
- 1 pound spaghetti, prepared according to package directions and drained
- 10 ounces sliced mozzarella cheese
- ¼ cup grated Romano cheese

Heat oil and butter in a large saucepan. Add onions and garlic and sauté until onions are golden brown. Add mushrooms, salt, pepper, oregano, tomatoes and basil. Add sausage and simmer for forty to sixty minutes, stirring occasionally. Place half of the spaghetti in an oblong baking dish. Place half of the mozzarella cheese over the spaghetti. Pour half of the sauce over cheese. Add remaining spaghetti, mozzarella cheese and sauce. Sprinkle with Romano cheese. Bake at 350° for twenty-five minutes or until heated through. Serves 4 to 6.

Manicotti with Mushrooms

- 1 pound ricotta cheese
- 3 eggs, lightly beaten
- ½ cup grated Romano cheese
- 1 8-ounce can mushrooms, drained
- 1½ teaspoons salt
- ¼ teaspoon pepper
- ¼ teaspoon garlic powder
- 1 pound manicotti
- 2 cups Meat Sauce (recipe on page 50), or use commercially prepared

Combine ricotta cheese, eggs, Romano cheese, mushrooms, salt, pepper and garlic powder. Mix well. Fill manicotti with above mixture. Place manicotti in ungreased baking pan. Cover half way with water. Pour Meat Sauce over top. Cover with aluminum foil and bake at 375° for one hour. Serves 4 to 6.

Rigatoni alla Chef

- ¼ cup vegetable oil
- 1 medium onion, minced
- 3 slices prosciutto ham
- 1 15-ounce can tomato sauce
- ½ cup Bechemel Sauce (recipe on page 52)
- 1 teaspoon salt
- ¼ teaspoon pepper
- ¼ teaspoon oregano
- ¼ teaspoon garlic powder
- 1 pound rigatoni
- ½ cup grated Parmesan cheese

Heat oil in a large frying pan. Sauté onion and prosciutto. Add tomato and bechemel sauces. Season with salt, pepper, oregano and garlic powder. Prepare rigatoni according to package directions. Drain. Place rigatoni on serving platter and pour sauce over all. Sprinkle with Parmesan cheese. Serves 4.

Noodles with Sour Cream

- ¼ pound noodles
- 1 cup cottage cheese
- 1 cup sour cream
- 1 egg, lightly beaten
- ½ teaspoon salt
- ⅛ teaspoon pepper
- 4 tablespoons butter, melted

Prepare pasta according to package directions and drain. Butter a two-quart casserole. Place pasta in a bowl and add remaining ingredients. Toss lightly. Place pasta in casserole and bake at 375° for fifty to sixty minutes. Serves 4.

Lasagna Casserole

- ¼ cup vegetable oil
- 2 cloves garlic, minced
- 1 medium onion, chopped
- 2 ribs celery, sliced
- 1 29-ounce can tomato sauce
- 1 6-ounce can tomato paste
- 1 6-ounce can water
- 1 teaspoon salt
- ¼ teaspoon pepper
- ¼ teaspoon oregano
- ¼ teaspoon nutmeg
- ½ pound Italian sausage
- 1 pound lasagna
- 1 pound ricotta cheese
- 1 cup grated mozzarella cheese
- ½ cup grated Romano cheese

Heat oil in a large saucepan. Add garlic, and onions and sauté for three to five minutes, or until onions are transparent. Add celery, tomato sauce, tomato paste, water, salt, pepper, oregano and nutmeg. Reduce heat and cook for one hour. Prick sausage with a fork and place in a baking dish. Bake at 375° for twenty-five minutes. Prepare lasagna according to package directions and drain. In a greased six-quart casserole, layer lasagna, tomato mixture, ricotta cheese, mozzarella cheese and sausage, ending with sauce and cheese. Sprinkle Romano cheese on top. Bake at 375° for thirty minutes, or until cheese is golden. Serves 4 to 6.

Spaghetti alla Gaetano

- 2 tablespoons vegetable oil
- 2 tablespoons butter
- ½ pound bacon, diced
- 1 medium onion, chopped
- ¼ teaspoon garlic powder
    Salt and pepper to taste
- ¼ teaspoon oregano
- 1 pound spaghetti
- 3 eggs, lightly beaten
- ½ cup light cream
- ¼ cup grated mozzarella cheese
- ¼ cup grated Romano cheese

Heat oil and butter in a large saucepan. Add bacon, onions and garlic and cook until bacon is crisp. Stir in salt, pepper and oregano. Remove from heat. Prepare spaghetti according to package directions and drain. Place spaghetti in a large bowl and add eggs, cream and both cheeses. Stir to mix. Add bacon mixture. Toss lightly and serve. Serves 4.

"Homemade pastas cook more rapidly than commerical. Begin checking for doneness after the first minute."

Alfredo's Noodles

   1 pound fettuccine
   ½ cup butter
 1½ cups sliced mushrooms
   1 teaspoon salt
   ¼ teaspoon pepper
   ¼ teaspoon oregano
   ½ teaspoon garlic powder
   ½ cup light cream
   ¼ cup grated mozzarella cheese
   ¼ cup grated Romano cheese

Prepare fettuccine according to package directions. Do not drain. Melt butter in a small saucepan. Add mushrooms, salt, pepper, oregano and garlic. Sauté for five minutes. Add cream and cook for two minutes, stirring occasionally. Drain fettuccine and place in a large bowl. Add mushroom sauce and both cheeses and toss gently. Place on a serving platter. Serves 4.

Farfalla with Fava

   2 tablespoons vegetable oil
   2 tablespoons butter
   ½ pound bacon, cut in pieces
   2 small onions, minced
   2 cloves garlic, minced
   1 16-ounce can fava or lima beans, with liquid
   1 pound farfalla
   ½ cup grated Parmesan cheese

Heat oil and butter in a large saucepan. Add bacon and sauté until crisp. Add onions and garlic and sauté until onions are transparent. Add beans and stir. Simmer over low heat for ten minutes. Prepare pasta according to package directions. Drain. Stir pasta into sauce. Add cheese and mix thoroughly. Serves 4 to 6.

Stuffed Shells

   1 pound large shells
   ½ pound ricotta cheese
   ½ pound spinach, cooked and chopped
   3 eggs
   ½ cup grated Romano cheese
   1 teaspoon salt
   ¼ teaspoon pepper
   ¼ teaspoon oregano
   ¼ teaspoon garlic powder

Prepare shells according to package directions, and drain. Mix ricotta, spinach, eggs, Romano cheese, salt, pepper, oregano and garlic. Fill shells with above mixture and place in a greased baking dish. Pour Fresh Tomato Sauce with Mushrooms over all (recipe on page 50). Bake at 375° for forty-five minutes. Serves 4.

Spaghetti Vesuvio

   ¼ cup vegetable oil
   2 tablespoons butter
   ½ pound sliced mushrooms
   1 teaspoon salt
   ¼ teaspoon pepper
   ¼ teaspoon oregano
   ¼ teaspoon garlic powder
   1 29-ounce can tomato sauce
   ½ cup sherry
   1 pound spaghetti
   ½ cup grated Parmesan cheese

Heat oil and butter in a large saucepan. Add mushrooms and sauté for five to seven minutes. Add salt, pepper, oregano and garlic powder. Stir in tomato sauce. Cook over low heat for two hours. Stir in sherry fifteen minutes before sauce is done. Prepare spaghetti according to package directions and drain. Place on a large serving platter. Spoon on sauce and sprinkle with cheese. Serves 4.

Fettuccine with Ricotta Sauce

   2 tablespoons vegetable oil
   2 tablespoons butter
   2 medium onions, chopped
   3 cups ricotta cheese
   1 8-ounce can tomato sauce
   1 6-ounce can tomato paste
   1 6-ounce can water
   1 teaspoon salt
   ¼ teaspoon pepper
   ¼ teaspoon oregano
   ¼ teaspoon garlic powder
   1 pound fettuccini
   ½ cup grated Romano cheese

Heat oil and butter in a large saucepan. Add onions and sauté over moderate heat until transparent. Stir in ricotta, tomato sauce, tomato paste and water. Season with salt, pepper, oregano and garlic powder. Reduce heat and cook for one hour. Prepare fettuccini according to package directions. Drain and place on a serving platter. Pour ricotta sauce over pasta. Sprinkle Romano cheese on top. Serves 4.

"Use your leftover cooked pasta in homemade soups and salads."

Ziti with Asparagus

1½ pounds asparagus, cleaned and trimmed
3 tablespoons butter
   Salt and pepper to taste
2½ tablespoons olive oil
2 cloves garlic
2 cups Italian plum tomatoes, pressed through a sieve
1 tablespoon chopped parsley
1 teaspoon basil
1 pound ziti
2 eggs, plus 1 egg yolk, lightly beaten
½ cup grated Parmesan cheese

Heat oil in a deep saucepan and add the garlic. Brown garlic and then discard. Add tomatoes, parsley, basil, salt and pepper. Cook, for about ten minutes, stirring frequently. Prepare pasta according to package directions. Just before pasta is done, remove tomatoes from heat and vigorously stir in eggs. Add asparagus and stir well. Drain pasta. Add tomato sauce and asparagus to pasta along with half of the cheese. Toss lightly. Serve with remaining cheese on the side. Serves 6 to 8.

Turkey Tetrazzini

½ pound spaghetti
2 to 3 cups shredded cooked turkey
1 pound mushrooms, sliced
4 tablespoons butter
3 tablespoons dry white wine
3 tablespoons butter
2 tablespoons flour
2 cups chicken broth
   Salt and pepper to taste
1 cup heavy cream
½ cup grated Parmesan cheese

Prepare pasta according to package directions and drain. Place turkey in a small bowl. Melt the four tablespoons butter in a small saucepan. Add wine and mushrooms and sauté for five minutes. Add to pasta and toss lightly. In a small saucepan add the three tablespoons butter, flour, broth and seasonings. Cook over moderate heat until thickened, stirring frequently. Remove from heat and stir in cream. Pour half of the sauce over the turkey. Pour the remaining sauce over the mushrooms and pasta. Place pasta in a greased baking dish. Form a hole in the center of the pasta. Place turkey in center. Sprinkle on cheese. Bake at 375° for thirty minutes, or until thoroughly heated. Serves 6 to 8.

Clam and Lemon Spaghetti

½ cup butter
3 tablespoons vegetable oil
1 medium onion, minced
2 cloves garlic, minced
2 8-ounce cans clams, drained and minced, reserve liquid
3 tablespoons lemon juice
1 tablespoon chopped parsley
1 tablespoon grated lemon rind
¼ teaspoon pepper
1 bay leaf
1 pound spaghetti
½ cup grated Parmesan cheese
   Lemon wedges

Heat three tablespoons of the butter and the oil in a medium-size, heavy saucepan. Add onions and garlic and sauté until golden. Add clam liquid, lemon juice, parsley, lemon rind, pepper and bay leaf. Simmer, uncovered, until liquid is reduced to about one cup. Discard bay leaf. Stir in clams and heat thoroughly. Add remaining butter, stirring until melted. Prepare pasta according to package directions and drain. Place on a warmed serving platter. Pour sauce over pasta. Sprinkle with cheese and serve with lemon. Serves 6 to 8.

Vermicelli with Eggplant

5 tablespoons olive oil
2 cloves garlic, minced
4 cups Italian plum tomatoes
4 tablespoons tomato paste
¾ cup water
1 teaspoon granulated sugar
   Salt and pepper to taste
½ cup chopped parsley
½ teaspoon basil
1½ pounds eggplant, peeled and cut into ½-inch cubes
½ pound vermicelli
¾ cup grated Parmesan cheese

Heat one tablespoon of the oil in a large saucepan. Add garlic and cook, stirring, without browning garlic. Stir in tomatoes, tomato paste, water, sugar, salt, pepper, parsley and basil. Partially cover and cook for about forty-five minutes, stirring frequently. Heat the remaining oil in a large frying pan. Add the eggplant and salt to taste. Brown eggplant until tender. Add eggplant to the tomato sauce and cover. Simmer for thirty to forty minutes. Prepare vermicelli according to package directions and drain. Place on a warmed serving platter. Spoon on sauce. Sprinkle on cheese. Serves 6 to 8.

Sauces and Fillings

Marinara Sauce

2 tablespoons olive oil, plus oil
   from anchovies
1 clove garlic, minced
2½ cups Italian plum tomatoes, drained
6 anchovies, chopped, reserve oil
½ teaspoon oregano
1 tablespoon chopped parsley

Heat oil in a medium-size saucepan. Add garlic and sauté for four minutes. Slowly stir in tomatoes. Add anchovies, oregano and parsley; stir well. Bring to a boil and then reduce heat. Simmer, uncovered, for fifteen to twenty minutes, stirring occasionally. Yields approximately 2½ cups.

Tomato Sauce

¼ cup vegetable oil
2 medium onions, minced
2 cloves garlic, minced
3 ribs celery, chopped
2 carrots, peeled and chopped
1 teaspoon basil
1 teaspoon chopped parsley
1 29-ounce can tomato sauce
1 teaspoon salt
¼ teaspoon pepper
¼ teaspoon oregano

Heat oil in a large saucepan. Add onions and garlic and sauté until onions are transparent. Add celery, carrots, basil, parsley and tomato sauce. Season with salt, pepper and oregano. Simmer over low heat for two hours, stirring occasionally. Yields 3 to 4 cups.

Salsa Verde

2 cups fresh parsley
2 small potatoes, peeled and cooked
1 small onion, cut into pieces
6 anchovies
2 teaspoons capers
2 cloves garlic
2 teaspoons basil
¼ cup vegetable oil
1 teaspoon salt
¼ teaspoon pepper
¼ teaspoon oregano

Place all ingredients in an electric blender and mix well. Serve over the pasta of your choice. Yields 1½ cups.

Pignoli Sauce

½ cup pine nuts
6 tablespoons chopped parsley
1½ teaspoons salt
¼ teaspoon pepper
¼ teaspoon oregano
3 cloves garlic, minced
¾ cup wine vinegar
½ cup grated Romano cheese
4 teaspoons butter

Place all ingredients in a small saucepan and bring to a boil. Reduce heat and cook for fifteen to twenty minutes. Yields 2 cups.

Meat Sauce

4 tablespoons vegetable oil
2 tablespoons butter
1½ pounds beef chuck roast, cut into cubes
2 medium onions, minced
2 cloves garlic, minced
1 6-ounce can tomato paste
1 6-ounce can water
½ cup red wine
1 teaspoon salt
¼ teaspoon pepper
¼ teaspoon oregano
1 bay leaf
1 29-ounce can tomato sauce

Combine oil and butter in a large saucepan. Add beef, onions and garlic and sauté until meat is lightly browned. Combine tomato paste and water. Add tomato paste, wine, salt, pepper, oregano, bay leaf and tomato sauce. Reduce heat and cook for two hours, stirring occasionally. Yields 4 cups.

Parsley Butter Sauce

2 tablespoons butter
2 tablespoons finely chopped parsley
1 teaspoon salt
¼ teaspoon pepper
¼ teaspoon oregano
¼ teaspoon garlic powder
¼ teaspoon basil
½ teaspoon lemon juice

Combine all ingredients in a small saucepan. Simmer until thoroughly heated. Serve over fish or vegetables. Yields approximately ½ cup.

Sauces and Fillings

Bechamel Sauce

1 stick butter
1 cup flour
4 cups milk, heated
1 teaspoon salt
¼ teaspoon pepper
¼ teaspoon oregano
¼ teaspoon garlic powder
½ teaspoon nutmeg

Melt butter in a medium-size saucepan over moderate heat. Do *not* brown butter. Add flour and stir constantly until well blended. Add hot milk all at once, stirring constantly until mixture is smooth. Add salt, pepper, oregano, garlic powder and nutmeg. Continue cooking and stirring until mixture is thick and smooth. Yields approximately 4 cups.

Fresh Tomato Sauce with Mushrooms

½ cup vegetable oil
1 pound mushrooms, sliced
2 small onions, chopped
2 cloves garlic, minced
½ teaspoon basil leaves
1 teaspoon salt
¼ teaspoon pepper
¼ teaspoon oregano
10 Italian plum tomatoes, peeled and coarsely chopped

Heat oil in a large saucepan. Add mushrooms, onions, garlic, basil, salt, pepper and oregano. Sauté until the onions are transparent. Stir in tomatoes. Reduce heat and cook for one hour or until the mixture begins to thicken. Serve over the pasta of your choice. Garnish with grated Romano cheese. Yields 3 to 3½ cups.

Red Clam Sauce

¼ cup vegetable oil
2 medium onions, chopped
3 cloves garlic, minced
2 green peppers, chopped
1 6-ounce can clams, chopped, reserve liquid
1½ teaspoons salt
¼ teaspoon pepper
¼ teaspoon oregano
3 tomatoes, crushed
½ cup water

Heat oil in a medium saucepan. Add onions, garlic and peppers and sauté until onions are transparent. Add clams and liquid, salt, pepper, oregano, tomatoes and water. Simmer slowly over low heat for one-half hour. May be served over noodles. Yields 2½ cups.

Basic Brown Sauce

¼ cup vegetable oil
2 small onions, finely chopped
2 tablespoons chopped parsley
¼ cup flour
2 cups beef stock
1 teaspoon salt
¼ teaspoon pepper
¼ teaspoon oregano
¼ teaspoon thyme
¼ teaspoon garlic powder
1 bay leaf

Heat oil in a small saucepan. Add onions and parsley and sauté until onions are transparent. Stir in flour and brown. Add beef stock and bring to a boil. Add salt, pepper, oregano, thyme, garlic powder and bay leaf. Simmer for four to five minutes over low heat, stirring occasionally. Serve over steak, meat loaf, or roasted meat. Yields approximately 3 cups.

White Clam Sauce

¼ cup vegetable oil
2 tablespoons butter
2 onions, finely chopped
3 cloves garlic, minced
2 green peppers, finely chopped
3 tablespoons flour
½ cup milk
1 6-ounce can clams, chopped, reserve liquid
1½ teaspoons salt
¼ teaspoon pepper
¼ teaspoon oregano

Heat oil and butter in a medium-size saucepan. Add onions and garlic and sauté until onions are transparent. Stir in green peppers. Mix flour and milk together. Add to onion mixture. Stir until thickened. Add clams, liquid, salt, pepper and oregano. Reduce heat and simmer for fifteen minutes. Serve over noodles. Serves 4.

Shrimp Sauce

¼ cup vegetable oil
2 medium onions, chopped
2 cloves garlic, minced
1 teaspoon minced basil
2 teaspoons chopped parsley
½ teaspoon salt
¼ teaspoon pepper
¼ teaspoon oregano
3½ cups Italian plum tomatoes, undrained
1½ pounds shrimp, cooked and deveined
¼ cup grated Parmesan cheese

Heat oil in a large saucepan. Add onions and garlic and sauté until onions are transparent. Add basil, parsley, salt, pepper, oregano and tomatoes. Cook for one-half hour, stirring occasionally. Stir in shrimp and cheese, and cook over low heat for one-half hour, stirring occasionally. Serve over spaghetti or rice. Serves 4.

Asparagus Sauce

¼ cup vegetable oil
1 pound asparagus, cleaned and cut
   into small pieces
1 medium onion, chopped
2 cloves garlic, minced
1 teaspoon salt
¼ teaspoon pepper
¼ teaspoon oregano
1 29-ounce can tomato sauce
½ cup grated Romano cheese

Heat oil in a large saucepan. Add asparagus, onions, garlic, salt, pepper and oregano. Sauté for ten minutes over low heat. Stir in tomato sauce. Cover pan and simmer slowly for one hour, stirring occasionally. Place cooked pasta on a serving platter and spoon on sauce. Sprinkle with Romano cheese. Serves 4.

Fillings

Chicken and Spinach Filling

2 tablespoons butter
¼ cup finely chopped onion
1 pound mushrooms, chopped
1 cup cooked spinach, drained and chopped
2 cups minced leftover white chicken meat
¼ teaspoon oregano
   Salt and pepper to taste
¾ cup ricotta cheese
2 tablespoons heavy cream

Heat butter in a small saucepan. Add onions and mushrooms and sauté lightly. Add the spinach, chicken, oregano and salt and pepper. Simmer for approximately five minutes. Remove from heat and cool slightly. Add ricotta cheese and cream. Mix thoroughly. Add seasonings to taste. Yields approximately 3½ to 4 cups.

Raisin Filling

1 pound ricotta cheese
3 eggs, lightly beaten
1 cup raisins
¼ teaspoon nutmeg
1 cup grated Romano cheese
1 teaspoon salt
¼ teaspoon pepper

Combine all ingredients and mix thoroughly.

Veal Filling

3 tablespoons vegetable oil
1 medium onion, chopped
2 cloves garlic, minced
1 tablespoon chopped parsley
1 teaspoon salt
½ cup ground veal
¼ teaspoon pepper
¼ teaspoon nutmeg
¼ teaspoon oregano
½ cup chopped celery
¼ teaspoon basil
½ cup Bechamel Sauce (recipe on page 52)

Heat oil in a large frying pan. Add onions, garlic, parsley, salt, veal, pepper, nutmeg, oregano, celery and basil. Simmer over low heat for five to seven minutes. Add Bechamel Sauce and stir well. Yields 1½ cups.

Beef and Tomato Filling

2 tablespoons butter
1 clove garlic, minced
1 small onion, minced
½ pound ground beef
1 medium tomato, chopped
1 teaspoon salt
½ teaspoon garlic powder
¼ teaspoon oregano
   Minced parsley to taste

Heat butter in a small saucepan. Add tomato, salt, garlic, oregano and parsley. Cook over medium heat for five minutes. Drain any liquid. Cool. Yields approximately 3½ to 4 cups.

Bread and Pizza

Great satisfaction can be derived from bread-making, but this art requires patience and some practice. If you are unfamiliar with the basic breadmaking process, but would like to try it, read the instructions below and then try your hand at the following bread and pizza recipes.

1   Dissolve yeast in warm, not hot, water (110-115°). Mix all ingredients thoroughly until dough is too stiff to stir.

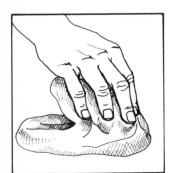

2   After flour is stirred in, turn dough out onto a floured board and knead by folding dough in half and pushing away from you.

3   Press with heels of hands and, pushing dough forward, continue to knead until dough is smooth and elastic, about eight minutes.

4   Test to see if dough has been kneaded long enough by pressing two fingers into dough. If it springs back, it is ready. Place dough in a greased bowl and coat top of dough with shortening. Cover and let rise in a warm place until doubled in bulk. Punch dough down and proceed with baking instructions.

Casserole Ricotta Bread

      1   package dry yeast
    ½   cup warm water (110-115°)
      1   teaspoon vegetable oil
      2   cups ricotta cheese
   2½   cups flour
      2   teaspoons granulated sugar
      1   teaspoon salt
    ¼   cup grated onion
      2   teaspoons anise seed
      1   egg
    ¼   teaspoon baking soda
      1   tablespoon butter, melted

Dissolve yeast in water. Combine remaining ingredients in a large bowl. Add yeast and stir until stiff. Turn out onto a floured board and knead until smooth and elastic. Cover and let rise in a warm place until doubled in bulk. Punch dough down. Shape into a round loaf and place in a greased casserole dish or a nine-inch round cake pan. Let rise in a warm place for thirty minutes. Bake at 375° for forty-five minutes or until bread makes a hollow sound when tapped lightly. Yields 1 loaf.

Bread Sticks

      1   package dry yeast
    ½   cup warm water (110-115°)
      2   cups flour
    ½   teaspoon salt
    ¼   cup sesame, poppy or caraway seed
      1   egg, beaten with 1 teaspoon water
          Sesame, poppy or caraway seed

Dissolve yeast in warm water; add oil. Place flour in a large bowl and add salt, and seed. Mix well. Add yeast, and mix well. If necessary, add more flour or water to make a stiff dough. Turn dough out onto a floured board and knead until smooth and elastic. Place in a greased bowl and coat top of dough with shortening. Cover and let rise in a warm place until doubled in bulk. Divide dough in half. Tear off pieces of dough and roll into sticks approximately ten inches long and one-half inch thick. Place bread sticks approximately one inch apart on a greased baking sheet. Cover and let rise in a warm place for twenty minutes. Brush egg and water mixture over bread sticks. Sprinkle with additional sesame, poppy or caraway seed. Bake at 350° for fifteen to twenty minutes. Yields approximately 2 dozen bread sticks.

Casserole Ricotta Bread
Carrot Bread, p.56

Bread and Pizza

Panettone

- 2 packages dry yeast
- ½ cup warm water (110°-115°)
- ⅓ cup granulated sugar
- 4 eggs, lightly beaten
- ½ cup butter, melted
- 1 teaspoon salt
- 1 teaspoon vanilla
- 1 tablespoon grated lemon peel
- 1 tablespoon grated orange peel
- 4 cups flour
- ½ cup light raisins
- ½ cup dark raisins
- ½ cup chopped candied citron
- ½ cup chopped pecans
- Melted butter

Dissolve yeast in water. Add sugar. Stir in eggs, butter, salt, vanilla, lemon and orange peel. Stir in remaining ingredients, except butter. Mix until dough is stiff. Turn dough out onto a floured board and knead until smooth and elastic. Place in a well-greased one- or two-pound coffee can. Brush tops with melted butter. Cover and let rise in a warm place for one hour or until doubled in bulk. Preheat oven to 375°. Bake for thirty-five to forty-five minutes for a one-pound can; forty to fifty minutes for a two-pound can. Cool in can for fifteen minutes before removing to a wire rack. Drizzle on glaze when cool.

Glaze

- 1 cup confectioners' sugar
- 2 tablespoons warm water
- 1 teaspoon vanilla
- Maraschino cherries

Combine first three ingredients and mix until smooth. Spread on panettone. Decorate with cherries.

Easter Bread

- 2 packages dry yeast
- 2 cups warm water
- 8 cups flour
- 1 teaspoon salt
- 1⅓ cups granulated sugar
- 2 teaspoons cinnamon
- Grated rind of 1 orange
- Grated rind of 1 lemon
- 2 tablespoons vanilla
- 1 cup butter, melted and cooled
- 6 eggs, lightly beaten

Dissolve yeast in warm water. Combine flour, salt, sugar, cinnamon, lemon and orange rinds and vanilla in a large mixing bowl. Add yeast, butter and eggs and knead well. Add more warm water, if necessary. Knead until soft and elastic. Cover and let rise in a warm place until double in bulk. Punch down. Shape into two or three round loaves. Place on a greased baking sheet. Cover and let rise until double in bulk. Brush with a beaten egg and bake at 375° for forty minutes or until golden brown. Yields 2 to 3 loaves.

Italian Bread

- 2 packages dry yeast
- 1½ cups warm water (110-115°)
- 2 tablespoons vegetable oil
- 4½ cups flour
- 1½ teaspoons salt
- 1½ teaspoons granulated sugar

Dissolve yeast in warm water; add oil. Combine flour, salt and sugar in a large bowl. Add yeast and mix well. Turn dough out onto a floured board and knead until smooth and elastic. Place dough in a greased bowl, coat dough with shortening and cover. Let rise in a warm place until doubled in bulk. Punch down. Divide dough in half and place on a greased baking sheet. Let rest for ten minutes. Mist top of bread with water. Place in preheated 400° oven for five minutes. Remove and spray again. Reduce heat to 375° and bake for thirty-five minutes or until golden brown. Yields 2 loaves.

Italian Bread Doughnuts

- 1 package dry yeast
- 1½ cups warm water (110°-115°)
- 3 tablespoons oil
- 1 teaspoon salt
- 3 cups flour
- ½ cup granulated sugar
- 1 teaspoon cinnamon

Dissolve yeast in warm water. Add oil. In a separate bowl combine salt, flour, sugar and cinnamon. Add yeast and oil to flour mixture and stir until dough becomes stiff. Turn out onto a floured board and knead dough until smooth and elastic. Place in a greased bowl, cover with a cloth and let rise in a warm place until double in bulk. Punch down. Break off pieces of dough and roll into balls two and one-half inches in diameter. Poke thumbs through dough and stretch into doughnut shape. Fill a frying pan half full of oil. When oil is hot, add a few doughnuts and fry on both sides until golden brown. Remove from oil and drain on paper toweling. Sprinkle with sugar. Yields 1½ dozen.

"Make your own bread crumbs by drying stale bread on a baking sheet in the oven. Grate dried bread and store in a covered container in the refrigerator."

Easter Egg Bread

    4 cups flour
  1½ cups granulated sugar
    1 teaspoon salt
    4 teaspoons baking powder
    1 cup shortening
    4 eggs
    ½ cup milk
    1 tablespoon vanilla
    8 hard-cooked eggs, dyed
      Multicolored cake decorating sprinkles

Combine flour, sugar, salt and baking powder in a large bowl. Cut in shortening. In a separate bowl, combine eggs, milk and vanilla. Add eggs to flour and mix until dough forms a ball. Add more flour or milk if necessary. Divide dough in half. Cover unused portion of dough. Divide dough into thirds. Roll into ropes approximately fifteen inches long and two inches wide. Pinch the tops together and braid loosely. Form into a ring and pinch ends together. Place braided ring in a greased bundt pan. Place four of the dyed eggs on top, spacing evenly. Repeat procedure for remaining dough and dyed eggs. Place in a preheated 375° oven and bake for thirty to forty minutes, or until golden. Cool in pans. Frost and decorate with sprinkles.

Frosting

    2 cups confectioners' sugar
    ¼ cup warm water
    4 tablespoons butter, softened
    1 teaspoon vanilla

Combine all ingredients and mix until smooth.

Carrot Bread

    2 cups flour
    1 teaspoon baking soda
    1 teaspoon cinnamon
    ½ teaspoon nutmeg
    3 eggs
  1¼ cups granulated sugar
    ¼ cup vegetable oil
  1¼ cups grated carrots
    ½ cup milk
    ¼ cup chopped nuts

Combine flour, soda, cinnamon and nutmeg in a small bowl and set aside. In a large mixing bowl beat eggs and sugar. Add oil and mix well. Mix in grated carrots and milk. Slowly add flour mixture a little at a time, beating well after each addition. Stir in nuts. Grease a 9 x 5 x 2-inch loaf pan. Pour batter in and bake at 375° for forty to fifty minutes. Yields 1 loaf.

Prune Bread

  1½ cups prunes
    ½ cup granulated sugar
    ½ cup honey
    ½ cup vegetable oil
    1 teaspoon cinnamon
    ½ teaspoon cloves
    ½ teaspoon nutmeg
    ½ teaspoon salt
  2¼ cups flour
    1 teaspoon baking soda
    2 eggs
    ½ cup nuts

Soak prunes in two cups water for six hours or overnight. Drain, reserving one cup of the water. Pit and chop prunes. Place water, prunes, sugar, honey, oil, cinnamon, cloves, nutmeg and salt in a medium saucepan and cook for five to seven minutes. Cool. Combine flour and soda in a large mixing bowl. Add eggs and nuts and mix thoroughly. Add prunes and mix well. Pour into a greased loaf pan and bake at 375° for one hour. Yields 1 loaf.

French Bread Cheese Pizza

    1 1-pound loaf French bread, sliced ¾-inch thick
    1 29-ounce can tomato sauce
      Salt
      Pepper
      Oregano
      Garlic powder
  1½ cups grated Romano cheese
  1½ cups grated mozzarella cheese

Spread sauce on each slice of bread. Place slices on a baking sheet. Season with salt, pepper, oregano and garlic powder to taste. Sprinkle with Romano cheese; then mozzarella. Place under broiler until cheese is golden. Serves 4 to 6.

Basic Pizza Dough

1 tablespoon dry yeast
1 cup warm water (110-115°)
2½ cups flour
1 teaspoon salt
2 teaspoons shortening

Dissolve yeast in warm water. Place flour, salt and shortening in a medium-size mixing bowl and mix thoroughly. Add yeast to flour and mix thoroughly by hand. Turn dough out onto a floured surface and knead until smooth and elastic. Place dough in a greased bowl, cover and let rise in a warm place until doubled in bulk. Punch down dough. For thin crust pizza, divide dough in half. Roll dough out to desired thickness and place on a greased baking sheet or pizza pan. Yields 1 thick or 2 thin crusts.

Neopolitan Pizza

Basic Pizza Dough Recipe
2 cups tomato sauce
1 teaspoon salt
¼ teaspoon pepper
½ teaspoon oregano
½ teaspoon garlic powder
½ teaspoon basil
1 2-ounce can anchovies
1 4-ounce can pitted black olives, sliced
¼ cup grated Romano cheese
1½ cups grated mozzarella cheese

Prepare Basic Pizza Dough. Roll out dough to desired thickness and place in greased baking pan. Spread tomato sauce on dough. Sprinkle with salt, pepper, oregano, garlic powder and basil. Add anchovies and olives. Sprinkle with Romano and mozzarella cheeses. Bake at 400° for approximately twenty-five minutes, or until cheese is golden. Serves 4.

Pizza alla Variety

Basic Pizza Dough Recipe
2 tablespoons vegetable oil
2 small onions, chopped
2 cups tomato sauce
½ pound ground pork
1 teaspoon fennel
1½ teaspoons salt
¼ teaspoon pepper
¼ teaspoon oregano
¼ teaspoon garlic powder
1 cup sliced mushrooms
1 green pepper, minced
½ cup grated Romano cheese
½ cup grated mozzarella cheese

Prepare Basic Pizza dough. While dough is rising, place oil in a small saucepan; add onions and sauté until onions are transparent. Add tomato sauce and cook for ten minutes. In a small bowl, combine pork, fennel and one-half teaspoon of the salt. Mix thoroughly. Roll out dough on a greased baking sheet to desired thickness. Spread sauce over dough. Season with remaining one teaspoon salt, pepper, oregano and garlic powder. Sprinkle on meat mixture, mushrooms and green pepper. Sprinkle Romano and mozzarella cheeses over all. Bake at 400° for twenty-five to thirty minutes. Serves 4.

Bundt Pan Pizza

Basic Pizza Dough Recipe
¾ pound ground beef or pork
1 teaspoon salt
1 teaspoon fennel seed
Salt, pepper, oregano and garlic powder to taste
1 cup grated Romano cheese
½ cup grated mozzarella cheese

Prepare Basic Pizza Dough. While dough is rising, combine ground meat, salt and fennel seed in a small bowl. Mix thoroughly. Prepare Sauce (below). After dough has risen, grease a bundt pan. Punch dough down and divide into thirds. Roll each piece of dough out in strips approximately two and one-half inches wide and twelve inches long. Place one strip in the bottom of the bundt pan, making sure that the ends overlap. Spread with Sauce. Sprinkle on one-third of the meat. Season with salt, pepper, oregano and garlic powder to taste. Sprinkle on one-third of the Romano cheese. Add second strip of dough and repeat above procedure. Repeat for the last layer. When top layer is completed, sprinkle with mozzarella cheese. Bake at 350° for seventy-five minutes. Serves 6.

Sauce

2 teaspoons vegetable oil
1 medium onion, diced
1 29-ounce can tomato sauce
¼ cup finely chopped green pepper

Combine all ingredients and mix thoroughly.

Desserts

Chocolate Cannoli Rolls

¼ cup cocoa
2 cups flour
2 teaspoons granulated sugar
¼ teaspoon salt
2 tablespoons vegetable oil
3 tablespoons wine vinegar
1 tablespoon water
3 eggs
1 tablespoon water

Combine cocoa, flour, sugar, salt, oil, vinegar, one tablespoon water and two of the eggs in a large mixing bowl. Mix to the consistency of pie dough. Add more water or flour if necessary. Knead lightly until smooth and elastic. Divide dough in half. Form into rolls one inch in diameter. Cut into pieces one-half inch long. Roll each piece into a four-inch oval and place on cannoli tubes. Mix remaining egg with water and seal edges with egg. Fry cannoli in deep, hot oil until golden brown. Remove from oil and cool slightly before removing from tubes. Fill with a knife or pastry bag. Yields 2 dozen.

Filling

3 cups ricotta cheese
½ cup granulated sugar
1 teaspoon cinnamon
¼ cup semi-sweet chocolate pieces

Combine all ingredients in a mixing bowl and mix thoroughly.

Persimmon Cookies

1 cup granulated sugar
½ cup firmly-packed brown sugar
¾ cup butter
2 eggs
¾ cup persimmon pulp
1 teaspoon vanilla
3 cups flour
1½ teaspoons baking powder
1½ teaspoons baking soda
1½ teaspoons cinnamon
1 teaspoon nutmeg
½ teaspoon cloves
½ teaspoon salt

Combine the first six ingredients and blend well. Sift together dry ingredients. Combine liquid with dry ingredients and mix well. Drop by teaspoonsful onto ungreased baking sheets and bake at 350° for twenty minutes. Yields approximately 6 dozen.

Amaretti Cookies

4 egg whites
½ teaspoon salt
2 cups granulated sugar
½ cup ground blanched almonds
1 teaspoon almond extract

Beat egg whites and salt together until stiff, adding sugar a little at a time. Fold in almonds and almond extract. Place by teaspoonful one-inch apart on a greased baking sheet. Sprinkle with extra sugar. Bake at 375° for fifteen to twenty minutes or until golden brown. Yields 3½ dozen.

Italian Fig Cookies

4 cups flour
3 teaspoons baking powder
1 cup granulated sugar
½ pound butter
3 eggs
1 cup milk
1 teaspoon vanilla

Combine dry ingredients in a large mixing bowl. Cut in butter. In a separate bowl mix eggs, milk and vanilla. Add to flour mixture and mix as you would pie dough. Roll out dough to one-quarter-inch thickness. Cut into five-inch circles. Place one teaspoon Filling in center of each circle. Fold circle in half and seal with fork tines. Place on greased baking sheet. Bake at 375° for twenty to twenty-five minutes or until cookies are golden brown. Yields 3 to 3½ dozen.

Filling

1 cup chopped walnuts
1½ cups chopped figs
1 cup finely chopped dates
½ cup granulated sugar
1 cup raisins
½ teaspoon nutmeg
1 teaspoon cinnamon
  Grated rind of 1 orange
⅛ teaspoon pepper
½ cup crushed pineapple
2 teaspoons light corn syrup
1 tablespoon whiskey

Combine all ingredients and mix thoroughly.

Almond Ricotta Cheesecake with Brandy

    2 cups ricotta cheese
    4 eggs
    ½ cup flour
    ⅓ cup granulated sugar
    2 cups milk
    ½ cup chopped almonds
    2 tablespoons butter, softened
    2 teaspoons brandy

Combine all ingredients in a large mixing bowl and beat until smooth. Butter a nine-inch round cake pan. Pour in batter and bake at 375° for forty-five minutes or until a knife inserted in center comes out clean. Yields 1 cake.

Zucchini Cake

    1½ cups granulated sugar
    4 eggs
    1 teaspoon cinnamon
    ½ teaspoon nutmeg
    ¼ teaspoon baking soda
    1 teaspoon baking powder
    2½ cups grated zucchini
    2½ cups flour
    ¼ cup vegetable oil
    ½ cup milk
    1 teaspoon vanilla
    ½ cup chopped nuts
    ½ cup raisins

Combine sugar, eggs, cinnamon, nutmeg, baking soda, baking powder and zucchini. Slowly add flour and mix thoroughly. Add oil, milk and vanilla. Mix well. Stir in nuts and raisins. Grease two nine-inch round cake pans. Pour batter into pans. Bake at 350° for forty to fifty minutes. Cool and frost.

Frosting

    3 tablespoons butter, softened
    1 teaspoon vanilla
    2 tablespoons hot water
    1 cup confectioners' sugar

Combine the first three ingredients thoroughly. Slowly add sugar and beat until smooth.

Raisin Cheesecake

    1 cup raisins
    2 cups ricotta cheese
      Grated rind of 1 orange
      Grated rind of 1 lemon
    1 teaspoon vanilla
    3 eggs
    1 cup flour
    ¾ cup granulated sugar

Soak raisins in hot water for ten minutes and drain. Preheat oven to 375°. Beat all ingredients together. Grease a nine-inch round or square baking pan. Pour in batter and bake for twenty-five minutes or until knife inserted in center comes out clean. Serves 6 to 8.

Carrot Cake

    2½ cups flour
    1½ teaspoons baking soda
    1½ cups granulated sugar
    1 teaspoon baking powder
    1½ teaspoons cinnamon
    1 teaspoon salt
    ½ cup vegetable oil
    1 teaspoon vanilla
    ½ cup milk
    1½ cups grated carrots
    2 eggs
    ½ cup finely chopped walnuts

Combine dry ingredients and set aside. Combine oil, vanilla, milk, carrots and eggs and mix well. Slowly add dry ingredients to liquid ingredients, mixing well after each addition. Stir in nuts. Pour batter into a greased 9 x 13-inch baking pan or a bundt pan. Bake at 375° for forty to fifty minutes. Cool and frost with Cream Cheese Frosting. Yields 1 cake.

Cream Cheese Frosting

    3 tablespoons butter, softened
    1 3-ounce package cream cheese, softened
    1 cup confectioners' sugar
    1 teaspoon vanilla

Cream together butter and cream cheese. Beat in sugar a little at a time. Add vanilla and beat until smooth and creamy.

Sponge Cake

    1½ cups granulated sugar
    5 eggs, separated
    2 cups flour
    ½ teaspoon salt
    1 teaspoon vanilla
      Grated rind of 1 lemon
      Grated rind of 1 orange

Beat sugar and egg yolks until very thick and yellow. Set aside. Beat egg whites until stiff, but not dry. Gently fold egg whites into yolks. Mix flour and salt together. Fold flour into eggs a little at a time. Fold in vanilla and grated orange and lemon rind. Butter and flour a 10-inch tube pan. Pour in batter and bake at 375° for thirty to thirty-five minutes or until a toothpick inserted in center comes out clean. Cool cake before slicing.

Italian Ice

    2 cups water
 1¼ cups granulated sugar
    1 cup orange, lemon, pineapple or
      cranberry juice
      Maraschino cherries to garnish

Bring water and sugar to a boil in a small saucepan. Stir until the sugar is dissolved. Boil for five minutes, stirring frequently. Cool thoroughly. Stir in juice. Pour into a freezer container. Place in freezer for four hours. Stir occasionally until mixture is almost completely frozen. Spoon into tall glasses and garnish with maraschino cherries. Serves 4 to 6.

Filled Peaches alla Milanese

    4 maraschino cherries
  ½ cup toasted almonds
  ½ teaspoon almond extract
  ⅛ cup confectioners' sugar
    2 peaches, peeled and halved
  ½ cup Marsala wine
      Whipped cream
      Maraschino cherries

Place cherries, almonds, almond extract and confectioners' sugar in a blender. Mix all ingredients lightly. Fill each peach half with above mixture. Place peaches in a small baking dish. Pour wine over peaches. Bake at 350° for seven to ten minutes. Garnish with whipped cream and maraschino cherries, if desired. Serves 4.

Baked Oranges with Fruit

    4 oranges
 2½ cups fruit salad, canned or fresh
    2 tablespoons kirsch
  ¼ teaspoon cinnamon
    3 egg whites
    3 teaspoons confectioners' sugar
    1 teaspoon finely chopped nuts

Cut off tops of oranges, scoop out pulp, remove seeds. Cut up orange pulp and add to fruit salad. Add kirsch and cinnamon. Fill oranges with mixed fruit. Beat egg whites until stiff. Fold in sugar. Spoon egg white meringue over top of oranges. Sprinkle nuts over all. Place in preheated 350° oven for five minutes, or until meringue is golden brown. Serves 4.

Fruit Compote

  ¾ cup granulated sugar
  ¼ cup water
    1 slice lemon
    3 tablespoons Marsala wine
    1 pint red raspberries
    2 peaches, peeled and sliced
      Whipped cream

Combine sugar, water and lemon slice in a small saucepan. Cook over moderate heat for about ten minutes, stirring frequently. Add wine and mix well. Pour syrup over raspberries and peaches. Cover and chill for about four hours. Serve with whipped cream. Serves 4.

Vermicelli Dessert

    1 tablespoon seedless light raisins
  ½ cup water
    4 tablespoons butter
  ½ cup cashew nuts
  ½ pound vermicelli
    2 cups milk
    1 cup granulated sugar
    1 teaspoon vanilla extract

Soak raisins in water for ten minutes; drain. Melt butter in a medium-size saucepan. Add nuts and raisins and sauté for five minutes, stirring frequently. Remove nuts and raisins and set aside. Break vermicelli in half and place in saucepan. Brown lightly. Add milk and bring to a boil. Simmer over low heat for eight minutes. Add sugar and vanilla. Cook for two additional minutes. Add nuts and raisins. Serve while hot. Serves 4 to 6.

Sicilian Kiss

    1 cup hot fudge sauce
    8 scoops vanilla ice cream
    4 tablespoons chocolate mint liqueur
    4 tablespoons chopped walnuts
      Whipped cream

Place one tablespoon hot fudge sauce in the bottom of an ice cream dish or glass. Add two scoops ice cream and press down firmly into glass. Spoon on two more tablespoons hot fudge sauce and one tablespoon mint sauce. Garnish with chopped nuts and whipped cream, if desired. Serves 4.

Index

ideals

Mama D's Italian COOKBOOK